William H. Brearley

A Summer's Vacation at the White Mountains

Third season

William H. Brearley

A Summer's Vacation at the White Mountains
Third season

ISBN/EAN: 9783337316556

Printed in Europe, USA, Canada, Australia, Japan

Cover: Foto ©Andreas Hilbeck / pixelio.de

More available books at **www.hansebooks.com**

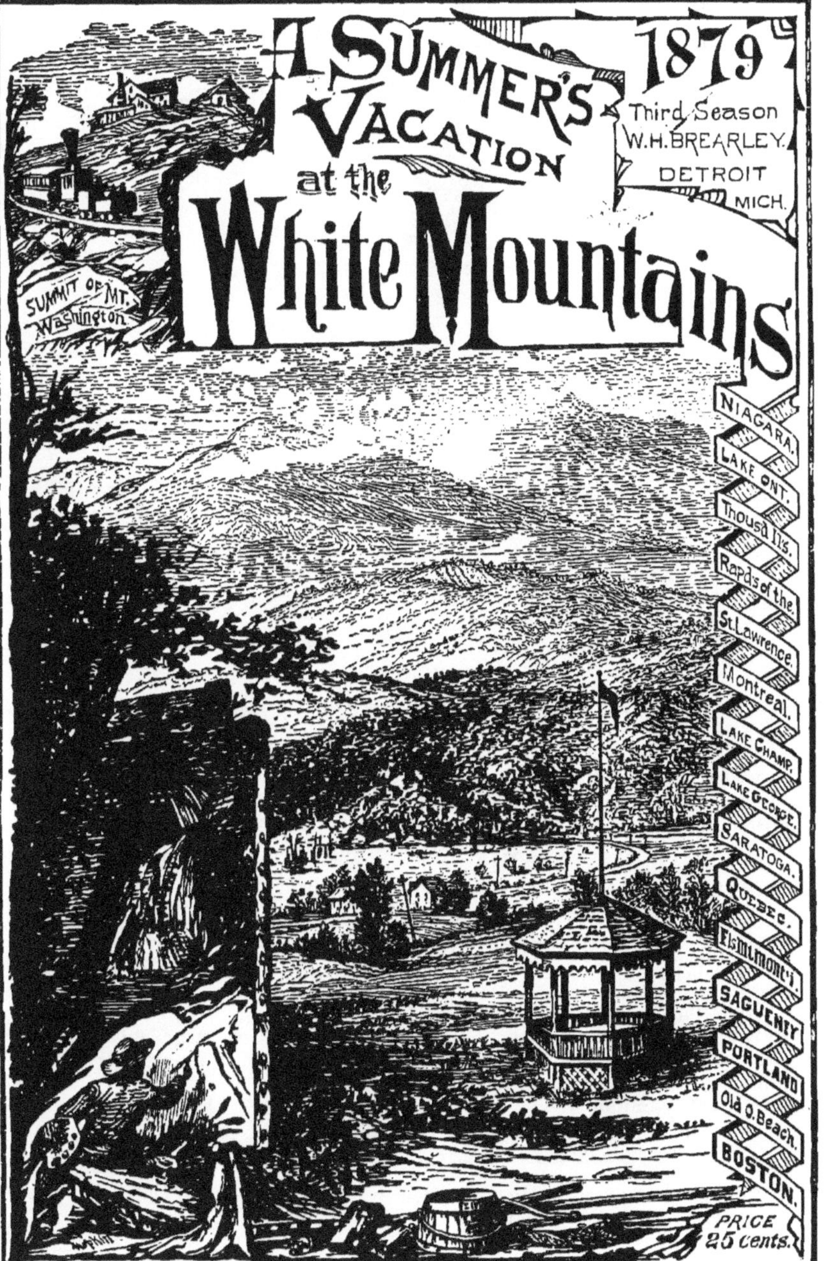

A Summer's Vacation at the White Mountains
1879
Third Season
W.H. BREARLEY.
DETROIT
MICH.
SUMMIT OF MT. Washington
NIAGARA.
LAKE ONT.
Thous'd Ils.
Rapids of the.
St. Lawrence.
Montreal.
LAKE CHAMP.
LAKE GEORGE.
SARATOGA.
QUEBEC.
SAGUENEY
PORTLAND
Old O. Beach.
BOSTON.
PRICE
25 cents.

THE EVENING NEWS,

DETROIT, MICH.

THE LEADING DAILY NEWSPAPER IN THE PENINSULAR STATE.

ESTABLISHED 1873.

☞CIRCULATION 22,000 copies daily—greater than that of all other daily newspapers in the State combined.

☞SUBSCRIPTION PRICE $5.00 a year, or 50 cents a month. Single copies 2 cents.

☞ADVERTISING RATES lower than those of any other paper in the United States of like circulation.

THE EVENING NEWS

Circulates over the entire lower peninsula of Michigan, being delivered regularly by carriers in 254 different cities and villages of this State and the adjacent counties of Ontario, Ohio and Indiana. As an illustration the circulation at a few points may be mentioned:

Ionia	101 copies.	Greenville	145 copies.
Big Rapids	110 "	Flint	235 "
Marshall	212 "	Battle Creek	325 "
Bay City	660 "	Niles	110 "
Pontiac	198 "	Mt. Clemens	100 "
Owosso	124 "	Port Huron	130 "
Adrian	195 "	Coldwater	170 "
Hillsdale	120 "	Charlotte	165 "
Albion	118 "	Jackson	210 "
Lansing	360 "		

With few exceptions THE EVENING NEWS has been the greatest journalistic success this country has ever seen. No Detroit paper exerts more influence both locally and throughout the State.

A weekly edition called

THE ECHO,

Is published every Thursday, at one dollar a year, or in clubs of two or more at 75 cents per copy.

BOOKS FOR SUMMER READING.

No.	Title	Cents.
1.	Is He Popenjoy? A Novel. By Anthony Trollope	15
2.	The History of a Crime By Victor Hugo	10
3.	The Russians of To-Day	10
4.	Paul Knox, Pitman. A Novel. By John Berwick Harwood	10
5	My Heart's in the Highlands A Novel	10
6.	Henriette. A Novel. By Earnest Daudet	10
7.	Christine Brownlee's Ordeal. A Novel. By Mary Patrick	15
8.	A Beautiful Woman. A Romance. By Leon Brook	10
9.	Honor's Worth. A Novel. By Meta Orred	15
10.	Kingsdene. A Novel. By the Hon. Mrs. Featherstonhaugh	10
11.	Cleveden. A Novel. By Stephen Yorke	10
12.	The People of Turkey. By a Consul's Daughter and Wife	15
13.	The Young Duke. A Novel. By Benjamin Disraeli (the Earl of Beaconsfield, K. G.)	15
14.	Haverholme. A Satire. By E. Jenkins	10
15.	"Bonnie Lesley." A Novel By Mrs. Herbert Martin	15
16.	The Rt. Hon Benjamin Disraeli, Earl of Beaconsfield, K G. With two portraits	10
17.	Selected Poems of Matthew Arnold	10
18.	The Bubble Reputation. A Novel. By Katharine King	15
19.	Among Aliens. A Novel. By Mrs. Frances E Trollope. Illustrated..	15
20.	Guy Livingstone; or "Thorough" A Novel By Geo. A. Lawrence..	10
21	Time Shall Try. A Novel. F. E. M. Notley	15
22.	Evelina. A Novel. By Frances Burney	15
23.	The Bachelor of the Albany. A Novel	10
24.	Auld Lang Syne. By W. Clark Russell	10
25.	Macleod of Dare. A Novel. By William Black	10
26.	The Mistletoe Bough Edited by M E. Braddon	15
27.	Rare Pale Margaret. A Novel	10
28.	Love's Crosses. A Novel. By F. E. M. Notley	15
29.	Light and Shade. A Novel. By Charlotte G. O'Brien	10
30	The Christians and Moors of Spain. By Charlotte M. Yonge	10
31.	Elinor Dryden. A Novel. By Katharine S. Macquoid	20
32.	The Irish Bar: Anecdotes, Bon-mots, Biographical Sketches, &c. By J. Roderick O'Flanagan	15
33.	The Last Days of Pompeii. By Edward Bulwer (Lord Lytton)...	15
34.	Through Asiatic Turkey. By Grattan Geary	15
35	Sport and Work on the Nepaul Frontier. By "Maori"...	10
36.	Jane Eyre. A Novel. By Charlotte Bronte	15
37.	An Eye for an Eye. A Novel. By Anthony Trollope	10
38.	Man and Wife. A Novel. By Wilkie Collins	15
39.	A True Marriage. A Novel. By Emily Spender	15
40.	Kelverdale. A Novel. By the Earl of Desart	15
41.	Within Sound of the Sea. A Novel	10
42	The Last of Her Line. A Novel. By Eliza Tabor, Author of "St. Olave's," &c	15
43	Vixen. A Novel. By M. E. Braddon	15
44.	Within the Precincts. A Novel. By Mrs. Oliphant	15
45.	All or Nothing. A Novel. By Frances Cashel Hoey	15
46.	The Plague in London. By Daniel Defoe	10
47	The Grahams of Invermoy. A Novel. By M. C. Stirling	15
48	Coward Conscience. A Novel. By F. W. Robinson	15
49.	The Cloven Foot. A Novel. By M. E. Braddon	15
50.	Quaker Cousins. A Novel. By Agnes Macdonell	15
51.	The Sherlocks. A Novel. By John Saunders	15
52.	That Artful Vicar. A Novel. By the author of "The Russians of To-day." &c	15
53.	Under one Roof. A Novel. By By James Payne	15
54.	Eothen. By Alexander William Kinglake	10
55.	"For a Dream's Sake." A Novel. By Mrs. Herbert Martin	15
56.	Lady Lee's Widowhood. A Novel. By Capt. Edward B. Hamley, R. A.	15
57.	A History of Our Own Times. By Justin McCarthy	20
58.	Basildon. A Novel. By Mrs. Alfred W. Hunt	15
59.	John Halifax, Gentleman. A Novel. By Miss Mulock	15
60	Orange Sily. A Novel. By May Crommelin	10

For Sale by **J. A. ROYS,**

WHOLESALE AND RETAIL

BOOKSELLER, STATIONER AND NEWSDEALER,

89 Woodward Ave., - - Detroit, Mich.

☞ Any of the above books will be mailed to any address on receipt of price.

TORONTO AND NIAGARA NAVIGATION COMPANY.

THE MAGNIFICENT CLYDE BUILT STEEL STEAMER

CHICORA !

Making daily trips and connections at Lewiston with New York Central, at Niagara with Canada Soutnern Railway, and

At Toronto with all Railroad and Steamboat Lines.

Tickets fcr Sale at all Ticket Offices of Connecting Lines.

For information as to rates, excursion business, etc., apply at offices,

B. CUMBERLAND,
35 Yongo Street, Toronto.

D. I. MILLOY,
8 Front street, Toronto.

DR. STONE'S TURKISH BATHS,

Boarding Accommodations
—FOR—
Invalids and Guests.

Street Cars from all the depots and principal hotels run directly past the

"CURE."

PERSONS visiting Detroit either for business or pleasure will find most comfortable rooms, with good board, at very reasonable prices, in one of the best locations in the city, at Dr. Stone's Turkish Bath House. Terms, including baths, not so high as at other first-class hotels without baths. Make this house your head-quarters when in Detroit.

274 Woodward Ave, } Corner Grand Circus Park, } **DETROIT.**

A SUMMER'S VACATION,

WHERE AND HOW TO SPEND IT.

THE ROUTE.

WHILE those purchasing excursion tickets can start on any regular train July 7th or 8th, the excursion proper will leave Detroit July 7th, at 11.10 P. M., by the Canada Southern Railroad, arriving at Niagara Falls the next morning at 8.30 A. M. Seven and a half hours will be given for seeing the Falls, and for breakfast and dinner at the International Hotel. Resuming seats in the cars of the Canada Southern Railroad at 4 P. M., the town of Niagara will be reached at 4.30 P. M., where the cars will be exchanged for the steamer Chicora, which after

CROSSING LAKE ONTARIO,

In the day-time, arrives at Toronto at 6.30 P. M., in time for the train east on the Grand Trunk Railroad, which leaves Toronto at 7.30 P. M (Montreal time). This train arrives at Kingston the next morning, July 9th, at 1.50 A. M., but the cars containing passengers for the St. Lawrence steamers are detached and backed down to the dock, where they remain until the steamer arrives from Toronto at 6 A. M The ride down the St. Lawrence, among the Thousand Islands and through

THE FAMOUS RAPIDS,

Will take all day, Wednesday, arriving at Montreal at 7 P. M., where the interval till 9.45 will be enjoyed by going to the Windsor Hotel for supper, and a short rest. In planning the route, it has been thought best to take the excursion direct to the White Mountains without stopping, and leave Montreal for the return trip, when time will be allowed for visiting it. There are reasons for this, one of which is that we desire to get to the Mountains in time to accommodate teachers who wish to attend the

AMERICAN INSTITUTE OF INSTRUCTION,

Which will hold its sessions July 8th, 9th, 10th and 11th. The excursion will, therefore, take the cars of the Grand Trunk Railroad at 9.45 P. M., arriving at Gorham Thursday, July 10th, at 8.50 A. M., where stages for the Glen will be in waiting. As the train reaches Island Pond at 5.15 A. M. (where breakfast will be taken), the mountain scenery between that place and Gorham will be passed in the day-time. The scenery passed between Montreal and Island Pond is of no special interest, and nothing will have been lost. Two days will be allowed at

THE WHITE MOUNTAINS,

As the excursion does not leave Gorham for Portland until Saturday morning, July 12th, at 8.53. This interval will permit of the ascension of Mt. Washington, and carriage or pedestrian trips to the various points of interest in the vicinity. The last two days' session of the American Institute of Instruction may also be attended, as described at length on page 37 in this book.

THE SEA SIDE

At Portland will be reached at 12.45 P. M. on Saturday, July 12th, where four days will be allowed, as the train for Quebec will not be taken till Wednesday, July 16th, at 2 P. M. This long rest is at the free disposal of the excursion. Special rates have been obtained at the Old Orchard Beach Hotel, 11 miles from Portland towards Boston, on the Boston & Maine R. R. No better sea-side resort can be found on the Atlantic coast, and all the privileges and novelties of the sea-side can there be obtained.

AN OCEAN VOYAGE

On a small scale may be made to Boston, by the Portland Steam Packet Company's steamers, which leave at 7 P. M. The distance, time required and accommodations are the same as on the Detroit & Cleveland line. By this plan you arrive at Boston Sunday morning at 7 A. M. Sunday and Monday can be spent there, and by taking the cars of the Boston & Maine R. R., which runs through Old Orchard Beach, this place can be "made" on the return trip. If this should be the plan, and you take the train from Boston Tuesday noon, July 15th, two days can be spent at the sea-side.

LEAVING PORTLAND

At 2 P. M., Wednesday, July 16th, the way is retraced by the Grand Trunk R. R. as far as Richmond Junction, where the road branches off to the right, terminating at Point Levi, which is opposite Quebec, and is reached at 6.45 A. M. Thursday, July 17th. The route between Portland and Island Pond, is again passed by daylight, and is all that is worth caring to see. The time at Quebec will be from the time of the arrival of the ferry from Pt. Levi, 7 A. M., to 5 P. M., when the steamer leaves for Montreal.

THE DAY AT QUEBEC

Is ample to visit all points of interest. The falls of Montmorenci, the little old French town of Beauport, the citadel and cathedral, and all other places can be visited, and these are the chief points of interest.

THE RIDE ON THE ST. LAWRENCE

From Quebec to Montreal will be one of the finest parts of the trip The steamers are as good as the famous Hudson river line, and as it is daylight until 8.30 P. M., the most interesting part of the river is passed before dark.

THE CITY OF MONTREAL

Will be reached Friday morning, July 18th, where a day or more may be spent in sight seeing. The city is of unusual interest to tourists.

THE RETURN TRIP.

The excursion will leave Montreal at 10 P. M. and return by the Grand Trunk R. R. to Detroit without interruption. Those living outside of

DETROIT

Should stop over, if possible, and visit the old "City of the Straits." It possesses many points of interest for the tourist.

THE DESIGN OF THE ROUTE.

The plan of the excursion comprehends some of the most beautiful scenery in the world, and the route by which these points of interest may be reached has been arranged with direct reference to assuring the comfort of the tourists. The frequent change from the railway to the steamer, and the return to railway, with stopping places interspersed, will remove the most objectionable features of traveling.

THE COOLEST ROUTE.

It should be remembered by those who desire to escape from the heat of midsummer, that much of this route is as far north as Lake Superior. The White Mountains and the sea-side, with the invigorating mountain and sea air, will give experiences not easily duplicated by a more southern route.

THE TIME FOR STARTING

Is Monday night, July 7th, at 11.10 P. M. This affords ample time for reaching Detroit from the interior of Michigan, or from almost any point in Ohio, Indiana or Illinois, without traveling on Sunday.

TICKETS.

THE tickets are $25 each, and are good for the round trip on any regular train.

CHILDREN HALF FARE.

Children over five and under 12 years of age will be passed at half fare. Children under five will be free.

ORDINARY RATES.

The rates quoted below are the regular ordinary fares *one way*:

Niagara Falls	$7 00
Toronto	7 00
Kingston	11 20
Montreal	15 00
Quebec	17 50
Gorham	18 00
Portland	18 00
Boston	20 00

This covers the fare one way only and does not include the stage fare at the mountains. The excursion tickets, however, are for the *round trip* and *include* the stage fare at the mountains, which ordinarily costs $8 extra.

WHERE TO GET TICKETS.

Tickets will be for sale at *five* places—the office of the Canada Southern Railroad, 153 Jefferson avenue (and at the depot, foot of Third street), also at the office of the Grand Trunk Railroad, No 156 Jefferson avenue, at the office of the DETROIT EVENING NEWS, 65 Shelby street, and at the Grand Trunk Junction. Persons from the interior of the State can stop off at the junction, purchase their tickets and join the excursion when it passes. Tickets *should* be secured in advance, however, by addressing W. H. Brearley, office of the EVENING NEWS, 65 Shelby street, Detroit.

WHEN TO GET TICKETS.

Send for your ticket *as soon as you have made up your mind to go*, instead of waiting till the last week. The reasons for this are many and important, especially to the manager of the excursion, who desires to learn, at as early a time as possible, the number intending to go. Tickets can be obtained up to and including the last day

—July 8th, but the manager would be *greatly accommodated* if an *earlier* date would be as convenient. A large number is not desired, and only a limited number of tickets will be sold. No tickets will be placed for sale outside of Detroit.

HOW TO MAKE REMITTANCE.

Any one of the three following methods of remitting money may be safely employed: Postoffice order, draft on Detroit or New York, or by registered letter. The name and address in full should also be enclosed that there may be no mistake in returning the ticket to the proper person, city and State. In remitting make drafts or orders, payable to the order of W. H Brearley.

EXCURSION CERTIFICATES

Will be sent free of charge to every purchaser of an excursion ticket, which will show that the holder is entitled to the special rates that have been obtained at hotels. As the certificates will have to be made out in the name of the holder of the excursion ticket, application should be accompanied with the name and address of each person.

SPECIAL RATES TO DETROIT.

Nearly every railroad centering at Detroit issues round trip tickets at reduced rates, from the various stations along their lines, to Detroit and return.

RUNNING TIME.

The various railroads centering at Detroit do not all arrive and leave this city by Detroit time. They run as follows:

Michigan Central R. R., Chicago time.

Michigan Southern R. R., Detroit time.

Detroit and Hillsdale R. R., Chicago time.

Flint & Pere Marquette R. R., Detroit time.

Detroit, Lansing & N.R.R., Detroit time.

Detroit & Bay City R. R., Chicago time.

Detroit & Milwaukee R. R., Detroit time.

Canada Southern R. R., Detroit time.

Great Western R. R., Detroit time.

Grand Trunk R. R., Chicago time.

The latter road changes its standard of time in various parts of its route, as follows:

Between Detroit and Port Huron, Chicago time.

Between Port Huron and Toronto, Toronto time.

Between Toronto and Island Pond, Montreal time.

Between Island Pond and Portland, Portland time.

ESTIMATE OF EXTRA EXPENSES.

These can be managed so as not to exceed $25 in addition to the ticket, or they can be as much more as you please. This estimate supposes first-class accommodations, in all respects, but does not include any unnecessary expense. It would be safer to take along *enough*, so as not to be embarrassed by any unforeseen emergencies that *might* arise.

The average expenses of last year's party were probably $40 or $50 besides the ticket. This is more however, than is necessary

EXTENSION OF TIME.

THE ticket proper is good to start on the 7th or 8th of July, and to return any time within 14 days, viz: on or before the 21st of July. Any one or every one, however, who will comply with the conditions upon which the extension certificates will be granted, can obtain one, free of cost, and with it can remain east 45 days, returning any time on or before the 20th of August.

The certificates will be given only to purchasers of regular excursion tickets and will be issued only by W. H. Brearley and upon the following conditions, viz.:

1st. That the holder will not sell or transfer the ticket, and

2d. That two photographs of the applicant shall be furnished; one to be mounted upon the certificate itself, and the other to be retained by the manager.

As the certificate can not be used without the photographs, the following suggestions should be noted: The photographs should be trimmed to a trifle less than

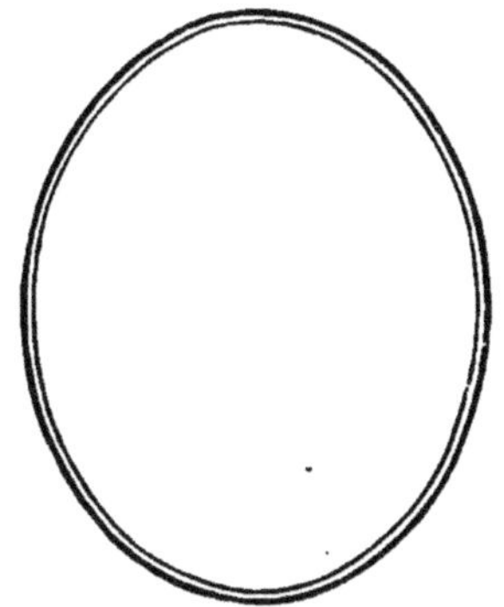

THE SIZE

Of the above oval. They should be un

mounted and covered on the back with mucilage ready to be moistened with the tongue and affixed without delay.

Photographs on cards will unfasten themselves without injury by being allowed to soak in water over night. Those having three or four days to spare in Detroit before starting may obtain the necessary photographs of the best quality and

FREE OF CHARGE.

At Randall's photograph rooms, No. 220 Woodward avenue. This offer is made in good faith and those who have purchased excursion tickets may feel perfectly free to avail themselves of the offer.

Forty-five days is the extreme limit to which any ticket can be extended. The certificates can be obtained either at the time of the purchase of tickets (when the photographs should accompany the remittance) or after the excursion has started.

SLEEPING CARS.

THE enjoyments of travel are greatly enhanced by the ease and comfort obtainable in the elegant Pullman or Wagner "sleepers." It is questionable whether it would be possible to put $5.00 where it would "do so *much* good" as to expend it in securing a berth for all the time that will be needed during the five nights of the fourteen days of travel. Where two travel together, and occupy the same berth, the price to each will be as above, but if berths are used by one person only, the price of course will be double. Sleepers from Detroit to Niagara Falls can be secured in advance by remitting $2.00 when excursion ticket is purchased. Sleepers for other portions of the route can be secured after starting, and at places stated elsewhere in this book. All trouble will be avoided, and the manager of the excursion will be greatly accommodated; if the following suggestions should receive deserved attention. Let those purchasing tickets remit for berths for the first night at the same time, and also state definitely whether they desire sleeping accommodations for the remainder of the round trip. In order that the manager can have time enough to make necessary arrangements by which sleeping cars shall be where and when wanted, and in sufficient number, it is *essential* that he should be possessed of this information as *early* as possible. There is no one thing that will contribute more to the comfort of the excursionist than this, and it should not be overlooked or forgotten. There is also no one thing that will be more appreciated by the manager than the courtesy herewith requested. No objection will of course be made to letting any one manage this for himself, and a surplus of sleeping car room will be provided for all such as well as for those who cannot purchase tickets until the last day.

SUGGESTIONS.

IT is the design of the following suggestions to answer questions and give reliable and needed advice. Any further information will be cheerfully given (if possessed) on application.

THIS GUIDE BOOK

Is intended to be used on the excursion, as well as to answer questions concerning the route. The places are described in the *order that they are visited.*

READ THE GUIDE BOOK THROUGH

All who go on the excursion should read this book through *before starting.* There are many things that are not touched upon in this preface that will be found in their proper places through the book, and in connection with the points of interest described.

YOU CAN GO ALONE.

Those holding excursion tickets can go and return by themselves, if they so desire, as the tickets are good to go on any regular train on July 7th or 8th.

LADIES TRAVELING ALONE.

No inconvenience or annoyance will be experienced by ladies traveling alone.

Last year there were several who *went* "alone," but did not *return* so, as it is impossible to resist the opportunities for making acquaintance, that so long a trip affords.

THE AMERICAN INSTITUTE OF INSTRUCTION

Will hold its session this year at the White Mountains, on July 8th, 9th, 10th and 11th, and promises to teachers a programme of unusual interest.

The "American Institute of Instruction" was founded in 1830, in Boston, and was intended, as its name indicates, to embrace the educators and educational interests of the whole country in its sphere of operations. Its membership embraces over 2,500 of the more prominent teachers of the country.

The morning session will commence at 9 A. M. and close at 1 P. M. The evening session will continue from 7.30 to 9.30 P. M. each day of the Institute.

In order to accommodate those desiring to attend the Institute, the route of the grand excursion has been so arranged that the 10th and 11th may be spent at the mountains.

A HANDY THING TO HAVE ALONG.

Dr. H. B. Drake, Homeopathic Pharmacy, at 228 Woodward avenue, Detroit, has prepared a small, neat case of Homeopathic remedies for the use of such of the excursion as are believers in Hahnemann. It contains the following 12 remedies:

1.	Aconite.	7.	Mercurius Sol.
2.	Arsenicum.	8.	Nux Vomica.
3.	Belladonna.	9	Pulsatilla.
4.	Bryonia.	10.	Phosphorus.
5.	Colocynth.	11.	Rhus Tox.
6.	Ipecacuanha.	12.	Veratrum Alb.

A book of directions accompany each case which will be found sufficient to guide the inexperienced.

These remedies are those most commonly used.

The price of case, with book, is $1.00, and will be sent to any address on receipt of price.

NO CROWD.

The time required for this trip and the price of the tickets will insure a choice company. There will be no crowd or rabble, no standing up or other difficulty. The only difference between this and other trains will be the addition of, perhaps, a couple of extra coaches to the regular trains. On the Canada Southern road, from Detroit to Niagara, the sleeping cars are Wagner's, on the Grand Trunk, Pullman's. By two joining together in securing berths on sleeping cars or steamboats, a saving of one-half is effected to each.

YOU CAN STOP OFF

At any point along the route either going or returning, and within the limits of the time allowed.

CHECKING BAGGAGE.

Trunks can be taken as in ordinary travel and without extra charge, but to avoid delay at the custom houses it would be well to check them from Detroit to Gorham or Portland. Only baggage from the States to some point in Canada, or vice versa, is examined. Ladies (who some ill-natured author describes as natural born smugglers) should make a note of this.

WHAT TO WEAR.

Ladies who seldom travel are sometimes at a loss what to wear or take for a long trip. The *less* baggage the better, usually, so it is best to wear something you are not afraid of spoiling and yet that looks well enough not to need changing. There is nothing better for a traveling suit than gray serge, which might be trimmed with the same, a contrasting color, silk or in any other of the numerous ways fashion allows this season. Of course gray serge is not by any means the only suitable material, and here as well as in the making and trimming, the figure, taste, and means of the wearer are to be consulted. A dress made of a material more easily soiled might be worn with safety if protected from dust by a linen ulster, and from rain by a waterproof. Apropos of waterproofs nothing could be nicer than the gossamer ones, now for sale at from $3 upwards, which are so fine and light that they take up almost *no* room, and are perfectly impervious to water. They are made of the finest rubber cloth and will last for years. Newcomb, Endicott, & Co., Detroit, have a large stock of them Many ladies will have some dress that they are not afraid of spoiling, and that will be suitable for traveling. In such a case it would be folly to have one made for the occasion. Of the two, it is much better taste to be dressed over-plainly than over-fancifully, in traveling. For a hat, anything that is plain, from which dust can be brushed and which a shower would not spoil.

Ladies who expect to spend the Sabbath in Boston or Portland, where they would wish to attend church, might wish to take a trunk, and if it is checked at Detroit to Boston or Portland there will be none of the annoyance of Custom House officials. Of course, one would naturally need little articles,handkerchiefs,brushes, combs, etc., where they could be easily reached, and a small hand bag would be needed for this purpose.

FIELD AND SKY GLASSES.

Every one who can possibly afford it, should secure a good field glass before starting. L Black & Co., opticians, at 77 Woodward ave., Detroit, have a very large stock at prices ranging from $3 to $25 They also have a great variety of spy glasses, at prices ranging from 50 cents upwards. This firm deal extensively in stereoscopic views, and no better resting place can be found in Detroit than at this store, where any who so desire can look over their views free of charge.

BOOKS, ETC.

Travelers often find some light reading very agreeable, and tourists often "wish they had thought to bring a note book," so that the beauties they see could be described on the spot, and the emotions they produced recalled as the notes are read afterwards. Such things as these can be obtained reasonably at J. A. Roys', 89 Woodward avenue, Detroit.

ORANGEMEN'S PARADE.

This excursion will not be in Montreal on the 12th of July, the annual parade day of the Society of Orangemen. If any of the party wish to be present at this, they will have to defer their trip to the Mountains for a few days. We spend a few hours here on our first arrival, the afternoon of the 10th, and do not return till the 18th.

OFFENSIVE AND DEFENSIVE.

The resolute intention of every excursionist will doubtless be, on starting, to preserve a strict conservatism, and to make no acquaintances among the other members of the party. The prediction is a safe one that this idea will be somewhat modified before the return. The first day this rigid decorum *may* be maintained, and probably *will* be. The second day it will suffer invasion at divers and sundry inevitable places. The third day, at the Mountains, there will begin to be felt that community of interest that always exists on a long voyage. This contagion will be spread during the succeeding days, by a natural and irresistible law of its own, until there will finally be an unexpressed understanding that will be akin to an offensive and defensive alliance.

PORTMANTEAU AND SHAWL STRAP.

One of the handiest and most convenient articles a tourist can secure is the combination illustrated above. Last year the manager of the excursion had no other baggage, and was *well* accommodated, as the portmanteau was large enough for collars, cuffs, brush, comb, razor and towels, while in the shawl straps were rolled a spring overcoat, blanket and duster; the whole forming a light, compact and convenient parcel. It is as ele-

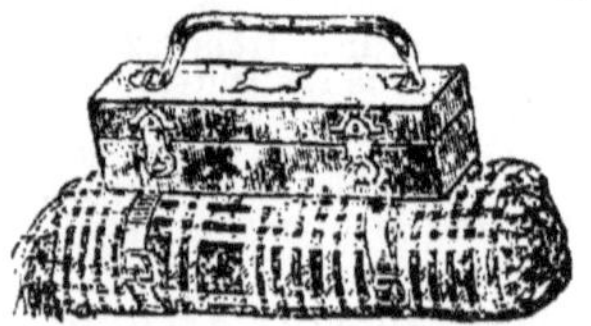

gant as a $10 satchel, more convenient and equally adapted for ladies or gentleman. It will be sent to any address on receipt of $2.00. Address (with P. O. order) the manager of the excursion, W. H. Brearley, 65 Shelby street, Detroit. Mich., and the goods will be sent by first express.

TIME VARIATIONS.

Owing to difference in longitude the true time will be found to be faster or slower than Detroit time, in proportion to the distance east or west of this city. The following table has been calculated for the convenience of those going on the excursion:

Buffalo, N. Y.—Fast 16 minutes.
Boston, Mass.—Fast 47 minutes and 56 seconds.
Chicago, Ill.—Slow 18 minutes.
Cinncinnati, Ohio.—Slow 6 minutes.
Cleveland, Ohio.—Fast 5 minutes.
Gorham N.H.—Fast 47 minutes and 35 seconds.
Grand Rapids, Mich.—Slow 11 minutes.
Kingston,Ont.—Fast 25 minutes and 30 seconds.
Montreal.—Fast 37 minutes and 59 seconds.
Milwaukee, Wis.—Slow 20 minutes.
Niagara Falls, Ont.—Fast 16 minutes and 12 seconds.
New York City.—Fast 36 minutes.
Toronto, Ont.—Fast 11 minutes and 38 seconds.
Toledo, Ohio.—Slow 3 minutes.
Quebec.—Fast 47 minutes and 22 seconds.
Portland, Maine.—Fast 51 minutes and 12 seconds.

MERE MENTION.

HEADQUARTERS for the excursion while in Detroit will be at the

BRUNSWICK HOTEL,

Corner of Griswold and State. The Cass avenue street cars, that leave the depot every five minutes, pass the door.

Those desiring livery while at Detroit may obtain the best in the city at

CASE'S LIVERY STABLE,

No. 40 Larned street west. This stable is connected by telephone with the Brunswick.

No one should start east on the excursion until he has selected some one or more of the

BOOKS FOR SUMMER READING

Advertised by J. A Roys, 89 Woodward avenue.

Several of the best engravings in this book were executed by the

WESTERN ENGRAVING COMPANY

Of Detroit, and fairly illustrate the excellence possible in wood engraving.

Several admirable sketches have been prepared for this edition by

ROBERT HOPKIN,

A Detroit artist. They appear on pages 43, 44, 52, 53, 55 and 56. The title page was also prepared by him, and represents the view from the piazza of the Glen House.

Dewey's Ice Cream, Oyster and Refreshment Parlors, Cor. Woodward and Adams Aves., is the only Ladies' Restaurant in Detroit. Ice Cream and Ices are furnished for Parties, Weddings, etc., and entire Suppers served. Catering in all its branches. Everything furnished guaranteed to be of the very best material.—WM. H. DEWEY, Manager.

All credit for the typographical appearance of this book is due to the MICHIGAN CHRISTIAN HERALD Publishing House, Detroit. The work compares favorably with the best that can be obtained in the city.

SIDE-TRIPS.

FOUR side-trips have been arranged, the price for which will be extra.

THE FIRST

Is from Groveton Junction to the Summit of Mt. Washington, and is described on page 37. The price will be $5 00.

THE SECOND

Is from Portland, Maine, by steamer on the Atlantic Ocean to Boston, and return by Boston & Maine R. R, stopping over at Old Orchard Beach. This route ordinarily costs $5.50. A special rate of $4.00 has been obtained for the round trip. For further particulars read pages 49 to 53.

THE THIRD

Is one of the cheapest and most profitable that can be found on the continent, being none other than a two days' trip (stated elsewhere inadvertantly as three days') by steamer from Quebec to, and up the famous Saguenay River to Ha Ha Bay and return. The price for this side-trip has been arranged for, at the very low low figure of $10, which includes all meals and state room. Full particulars are given on pages 57 and 58.

THE FOURTH AND LAST.

On the return trip, arrangements have been made to stop over at Montreal and "run" down to Saratoga and back. This route, which is fully described on pages 58 to 61, will cost $12.75 (and not $12.50 as stated on page 58). This side-trip will be found a fitting finale to the GRAND EXCURSION.

TICKETS FOR THE SIDE-TRIPS.

Will not be sold in advance, nor to any one but those holding the general excursion tickets. Full information as to when and where to obtain these tickets are given in connection with the descriptions.

SUMMER RESORTS.

GOOD PLACES TO SPEND THE SUMMER.

THE EVENING NEWS will by sent regularly to the following popular summer resorts during July and August, and will be kept on file in their reading rooms, for the convenience of Michigan guests, who desire to obtain home news:

Boston, ...Brunswick Hotel.
Bethlehem, N. H. ......Maplewood Hotel.
Bethlehem, N. H. ....Sinclair House.
Caconna, Canada, ...St. Lawrence Hall.
Franconia, N. H. ....Goodnow House.
Island Pond, Vt., ...Island Pond House
Jefferson, N. H., ...Waumbek House.
Lake George,..Fort William Henry Hotel.
Littleton N. H ....Thayer's Hotel
Manhattan Beach, N. Y. ....Grand Hotel.
Montreal, ...Windsor Hotel
Montreal.....................Ottawa Hotel.
Niagara Falls........International Hotel.
Niagara Falls...............Cataract House.
Niagara Falls ....Clifton House.
Old Orchard Beach. ... ...Ocean House.
Old Orchard Beach...Old Orchard House.
Plattsburg, N. Y. ....Forquet House.
Portland, Me..................Cape Cottage.
Portland, Me.............Falmouth House.
Plymouth, N. H...Pemigewassett House.
Put-in-Bay......................Beebe House.
Quebec.........................Russell House.
Quebec.... .. ..St. Louis Hotel.
Saratoga ....Congress Hall.
Saratoga..............Grand Union Hotel.
Saratoga..............United States Hotel.
Thousand Islands.......Crossman House.
Thousand Islands.Thousand Island House.
Toronto ....Queen's Hotel.
Toronto........................Rossin House.
White Mountains..........Alpine House.
White Mountains.......Crawford House.
White Mountains..........Fabyan House
White Mountains...........Flume House.
White Mountains..............Glen House.
White Mountains...........Profile House.
White Mountains ....Summit House.
White Mountains.Twin Mountain House.
Wolfborough, N. H.......Pavilion House.

INDEX.

A SUMMER'S VACATION.

Third Season. Cool Northern Route. Distance 2,000 miles.

W. H. BREARLEY, DETROIT, MICH.

Leaves Detroit July 7. Time 14 or 45 Days. Round Trip, $25.00.

THE OLDEST CITY IN THE WEST.

PONTIAC TREE, DETROIT.

DETROIT, the oldest city in the West, as well as the commercial metropolis and largest city of Michigan, containing 130,000 inhabitants, is beautifully situated on the Detroit river, 18 miles from Lake Erie and 7 miles from Lake St. Clair. Its eventful history and rapid development since the war make it a place well worthy the tourist's study and inspection.

HISTORICAL.

Upon its discovery by white men, the site now occupied by Detroit was the location of several Indian villages. It was first visited by the French, in 1610, and remained in possession of that nationality until 1762. The first legitimate settlement was made in 1701, when Antoine de la Motte Cadillac erected Fort Pontchartrain, the nucleus of the present city, naming the place D'Etroit (the strait)—hence Detroit—and became first governor of the territory. This fort was simply a square stockade with block-house corners, the northwest corner of which must have been very near the site of the front of the present Michigan Exchange hotel, corner of Jefferson avenue and Shelby street. It originally occupied but about the space of one of the present city squares, but was doubled in size about 1750, when the governor's house occupied the site on which now stands the First National Bank, corner of Jefferson avenue and Griswold street. In 1763 the British took possession, and soon had trouble with the Indians, who had been on quite friendly terms with the French. Of the several tribes in the vicinity—Pottawottamies, Wyandots and Ottawas—Pontiac, an Ottawa, was chief. His home was on Peach Island, near the Canada shore just above Belle Isle. Concluding that the British were inimical to his race, he decided to attack Detroit, and in July, 1763, was ready for business, and located with his warriors at Parent Creek, or Bloody Run. The garrison made a sortie, however, and advanced to attack the Indians. The latter lay in ambush, and when the Bloody Run bridge was reached opened a deadly fire that laid many of the attacking party low in death and drove the remainder back to the fort; entailing a loss to the British of 25 killed and 38 wounded. The only living witness of this bloody scene is the "Pontiac Tree," which may be seen to-day, old and scarred, on the Michigan Stove Company's grounds, in the Bloody Run hollow, a little to the right of Jefferson avenue going eastward, and about two miles from the center of the city: passed regularly by the Jefferson avenue street cars. In 1778 the British built fort Shelby on the site now occupied by Whitney's Opera House, corner Fort and Shelby streets.

OLD PEAR TREES.

The American flag first waved over Detroit in 1796, when the fort and town were evacuated by the British under the Jay treaty, and taken possession of by Capt. Potter of Gen. Wayne's command. It remained in American hands until Hull's surrender to Gen. Brock, Aug. 16, 1812; but the British only held it about 13 months, for on Sept. 28, 1813, the Americans under Gen. McArthur again floated their flag from the fort staff, since which time it has continued American, Michigan being admitted as a state in 1837, with Detroit as the capital, which it remained until the removal of the capital to Lansing, in 1847. The rear part of the present High School building served as the old State House.

OLD PEAR TREES.

The French soldiers who came over with Cadillac about the year 1700, brought pear seeds from Normandy, and planted them along the river front where they afterwards grew to be shade trees for the old French homesteads. All but a few of these venerable landmarks have been removed to make way for building improvements.

THE DETROIT OF TO-DAY

Will be a revelation to the tourist who has not visited the city for a decade or two. Its growth, especially during the past 20 years, has been wonderful. In that time it has about tripled its population by a natural, steady growth, not stimulated by any excitement, but accruing to the city because of its solid worth. The river at this point is about five-eighths of a mile wide, and on the opposite side is the Canadian city of Windsor, two miles below which is the old town of Sandwich, while two miles above is Walkerville, which takes its name from a leading distiller who has his grain-destroying factory located there. The harbor is really the most perfect on the whole chain of lakes.

As a commercial center Detroit ranks high, with her nearly a dozen lines of railroads centering here, and with others of large importance about to be brought to her to connect her with the great Southwest. There are but two great depots, however—at the foot of Third street and at the foot of Brush street—although of late, so far has the city spread, passenger depots 1¾ miles out Grand River avenue and two miles out Woodward avenue, have been found of great convenience. The State of Michigan is tapped in all directions by roads leading to Detroit, and great through lines pass their immense traffic oceanward through her confines.

Detroit is also emphatically a city of homes. Possibly no other city—not even Philadelphia—possesses as great a number of people, in proportion to its population, who own their own homes, and sit under their own vine and fig tree, as Detroit. And such homes—no cramped up, crowded blocks, but substantial, independent buildings, with plenty of light and air, and little bits of green about them to brighten and cheer the inmates.

The principal buildings are: The City Hall, of which every Detroiter is especially proud; a massive building of Italian style, covering a ground area of 200x90 feet, and 180 feet in height to the top of the central tower; built at a cost of $600,000, and without jobbery, else it would have cost much more. Two handsome opera houses—the Detroit, situated on the Campus Martius, one of the largest and best appointed theaters west of New York; and Whitney's, on the corner of Fort and Shelby streets, a perfect bijou of a theater, and yet not so small after all—both arranged with every regard for the safety and comfort of the public. The post-office, corner of Griswold and Larned streets, in which is also located the custom-house. Harmonic Hall, a handsome building erected by the Harmonie society from the proceeds of a lottery, situated on the corner of Lafayette and Beaubien streets, and devoted to music and the drama, terpsichorean gatherings, etc. Young Men's Hall, used for public gatherings, situated in the Biddle House block. There are also several other sizable halls. The High School building, corner of Griswold and State streets, a very handsome structure erected at a cost of $60,000. The Public Library building, on Center Park, Gratiot avenue, just off Woodward avenue, completed at a cost of $125,000, and with a well-stocked library of some 45,000 volumes, yearly increasing.

Of handsome business blocks may be mentioned the new Chandler block and Chamber of Commerce building, on Jefferson Avenue; the Moffat block, corner of Fort and Griswold streets; the Mechanics' block, opposite the City Hall, on Griswold street: the Williams block, corner Campus Martius and Michigan Grand avenue; the old Board of Trade, on Woodbridge street; the Telegraph block, corner of Griswold and Congress streets, and the Bank block, directly opposite; the Wayne County Savings bank on Congress street; the Weber block, on Woodward avenue, above the Campus; and scores of others that might be named.

THE RUSSELL HOUSE, (FROM CITY HALL STEPS.)

There are also plenty of good hotel accommodations. The leading house is the Russell, opposite the City Hall. Then there are the Michigan Exchange, corner of Jefferson avenue and Shelby streets; the Brunswick, corner of State and Griswold streets; and the Biddle (closed at present, because of an eccentric owner), on Jefferson avenue; also, good houses in the Cass hotel, opposite the Third street depot; the Antisdel House, on Michigan avenue; the Howard House, corner of Congress and Griswold streets; the Finney House, and others.

Street cars intersect the city in all directions. Of two lines leading from the depot of the Michigan Central Railroad, at the foot of Third street, one—the City Railway line—gives change-off tickets to passengers to take Gratiot, Michigan or Woodward avenue cars. And by this means the center of the city and the principal public buildings can be reached by it, as well as by the Cass avenue and Third street line. Then we have the Grand

River avenue line, the Fort street line through the entire length of the city, etc.

Public and private schools abound in profusion and there are church accommodations to suit all religions and all tastes. There are several leading hospitals, as the Harper, on Woodward avenue; St. Mary's, on Clinton street; St. Luke's, on Fort street west; the Woman's hospital and Foundling's Home, on Thirteenth street, near Grand River avenue; the House of Providence, an infant asylum and lying-in hospital, corner of Antoine and Elizabeth streets; the U. S. Marine hospital, out Jefferson avenue, etc There are a number of orphan asylums, the largest being St. Vincent's, a magnificent building on McDougall avenue, to the left of Jefferson avenue going east. Also a Home of the Friendless, on Warren avenue; deaf and dumb asylum, insane asylum, etc.

Detroit is not well off in the matter of parks, however. There are a number of little grass plots scattered about the city and dignified by the title of park, but wholly unworthy the name. Linden park (30 acres) just outside the city limits on the east, is wholly unimproved as yet; but a new park of 18 acres, to be known as the Recreation park, is completed and is quite handsome. Here are played the base ball games, etc. It is situated to the right of Woodward avenue, back of Harper Hospital, and is reached by the Woodward avenue cars

Other public works of Detroit, in which she takes great pride are her new Water Works, located beyond the city limits, in Hamtramck, out Jefferson avenue, on the river bank, erected at a cost of $1,000,000, and well worth a visit from any tourist, just to see the great engine work. Also, the monument erected to the memory of the Michigan soldiers and sailors who fell in the war for the union, 1861-65, designed by Randolph Rogers, and built of bronze and granite at a cost of $60,000 It stands 55 feet high, surmounted by a colossal bronze allegorical statue of Michigan, with the various branches of the service illustrated by life-size bronze figures on four corners. Also the House of Correction, on Russell street, erected at a cost of $300,000, and which has attained a national reputation as an ably managed institution, prisoners being sent to it from many states and territories. It has reached the point of self-support, and is well worth a visit.

DETROIT OPERA HOUSE.

THE CEMETERIES.

In the matter of "silent cities" Detroit is well supplied. Three large cemeteries are here, viz: Elmwood, Mt. Elliott, (Catholic) and Woodmere. The first two join each other on the eastern limits of the city, while the last is located on the river six miles below the city, and is accessible by carriage road or railroad. Woodmere, the latest, is a beautiful spot, and will in time be the leading burial place. The most accessible is Elmwood, beautifully situated naturally and so embellished artificially as to be well worth a tourist's visit. The Fort street cars going eastward will take you directly to the entrance gate. Here lie the remains of Detroit's most noted citizens—Gen. Lewis Cass and others. Here also is the firemen's lot and monument, and many other monuments and tombstones whose inscriptions will interest those who care to wander in the city of the dead. The historical Bloody Run passes through the cemetery, which is very handsomely laid out, and is well kept.

AN OLD LANDMARK.

A relic of interest to look at, as reminding one of the old French days of Detroit, is the Campau homestead, about the only old landmark in the building line left in the city. It is situated on Jefferson

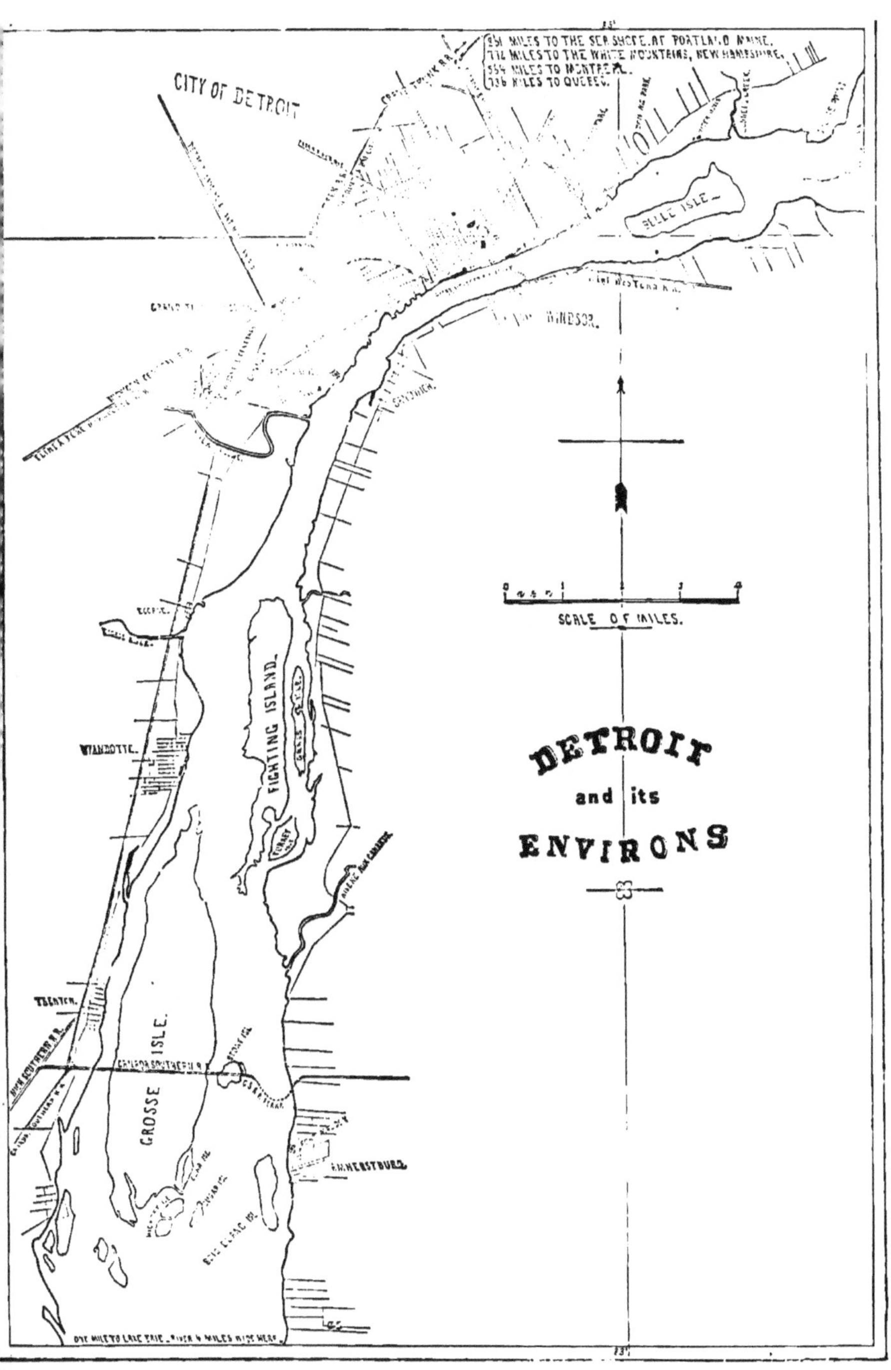

DETROIT
and its
ENVIRONS
CITY OF DETROIT
BELLE ISLE
WINDSOR.
SCALE OF MILES.
FIGHTING ISLAND
GROSSE ISLE.
WYANDOTTE.
TRENTON.
AMHERSTBURG.
ONE MILE TO LAKE ERIE _ RIVER 4 MILES WIDE HERE.

avenue near Griswold street, is 45x42 ft.in size, and built in the old French style. This quaint house, whose foundation was laid in 1750, but whose upper portion was destroyed in the great fire of 1805, and immediately restored, strikes the eye of every stranger visiting Detroit, standing as it does wedged in among the lofty business blocks of Jefferson avenue, with its upper and lower doors, antique latches, and odd little windows.

NEWSPAPERS, ETC.

Detroit is well provided with purveyors of current history. Besides a score or two weekly, monthly, and other publications, in English and German, it has two German dailies and three leading English dailies. The first in order of life and circulation is THE EVENING NEWS, with a circulation of 22,000 copies daily, issued from one of the neatest newspaper printing offices in the country, situated on Shelby street, just north of Larned. Next comes the *Free Press*, Democratic, issued every morning, with a circulation of about 5,000; and the *Post and Tribune*, Republican, issued each morning, circulation about 4,000. Job printing offices abound in all parts of the business center of the city, and printers' ink may be said to be generally appreciated by Detroiters.

DIRECTIONS TO SIGHT-SEERS.

The best comprehensive view of Detroit can be obtained by ascending to the City Hall tower and using a good field-glass. The broad avenues, lined with shade-trees; the splendid harbor, and the islands in the river; Fort Wayne, on the river below the city; and points of interest for several miles about, can be taken in at a glance in this manner. To those who have more time, however, and who care to "take in" more of the beauties of Detroit, a drive under care of an intelligent and obliging hackman (and there are such in Detroit, if you keep your eyes open for them) will be best. You can tell him to lay out the pleasantest route to such points of interest enumerated here as you care to visit, and make your bargain with him before starting. A party of four may enjoy this luxury for $1.00 an hour. Or you can go to the District Telegraph office, on Congress street, corner of Griswold, and order a coupe after having a route laid out, and indulge in this for 60 cents an hour. A coupe carries two persons. Or yet again, you can secure the aid of the obliging hotel clerk to lay you out a route, and order a carriage or coupe from the hotel. In fact there is no end of ways by which the tourist, having a day or two in Detroit, can profitably fill in his time at sight-seeing at reasonable rates.

In the summer season cheap excursions by water abound. You can go to St. Clair Flats to fish for 50 cents the round trip; to Put-in-Bay Island (the scene of Perry's resting place after his victory on Lake Erie in 1813), for $1 the round trip; to the Sandwich mineral springs, to Wyandotte white sulphur springs, to Mt. Clemens mineral springs, and various other points—all for merely nominal sums. The Detroit River is about 25 miles long, and from five-eighths to one mile wide, abounding in places for picknicking and pleasuring. A fine summer resort on Grosse Isle (the Alexander House) is in daily communication by boat during the summer, at cheap fare, and the evenings are lively with moonlight excursions.

LEAVING DETROIT.

THE EVENING NEWS excursion will leave Detroit, July 7th, at 11:10 P.M. by the Canada Southern Railroad from the depot at the foot of Third street. Those who prefer to go alone can use the excursion tickets and follow on any regular train the next day.

Sleeping car accommodations from Detroit to Niagara are $2.00 per berth or $4.00 per section. Two can occupy a berth, if they so desire, without extra expense.

THE FIRST NIGHT.

The route the first night is by Canada Southern Railroad, south to the crossing (by iron ferry) at Grosse Isle, thence east via Fort Erie, opposite Buffalo, to Clifton, near Niagara Falls. The approach to the Falls by the Canada Southern Railroad is particularly fine, as may be seen by the accompanying map. The road runs for some distance on the bank of the river, directly overlooking the Falls.

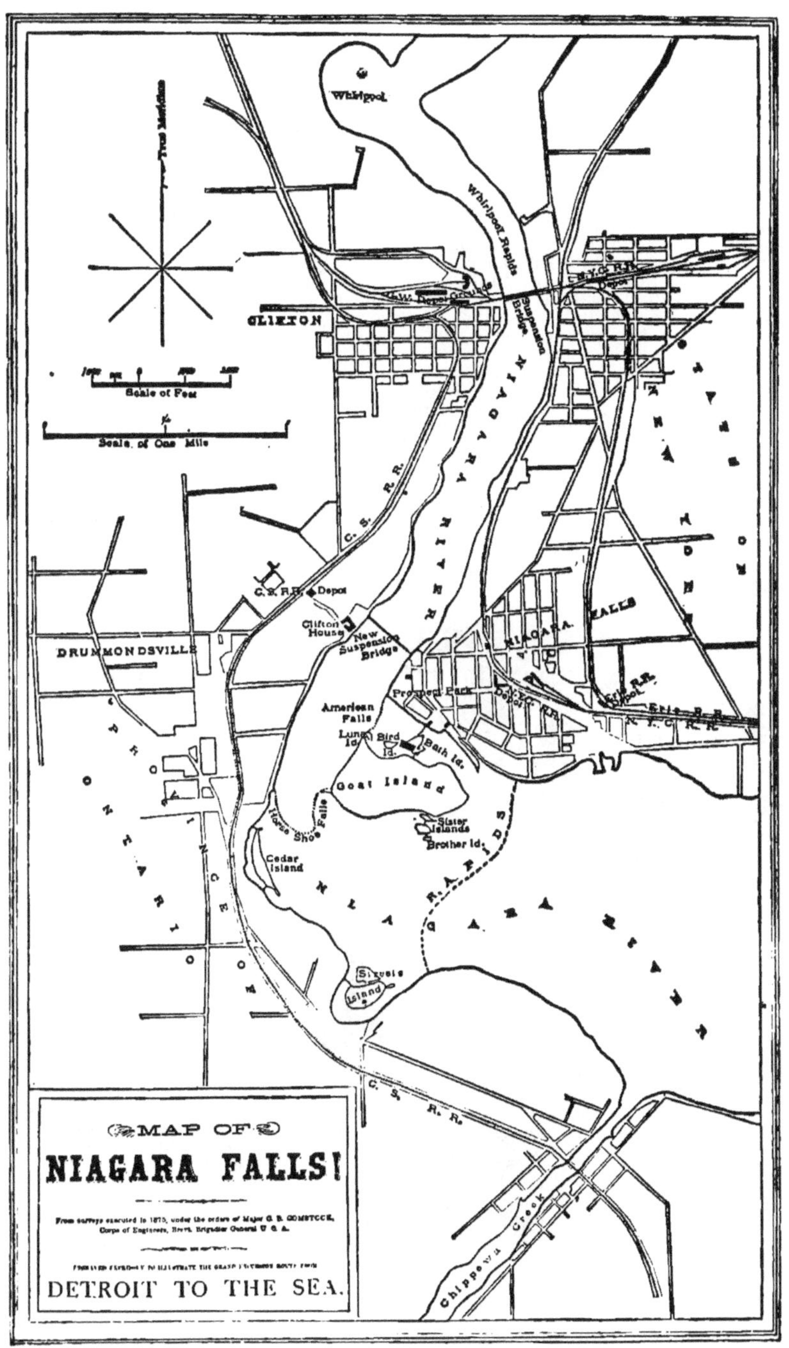

Whirlpool
True Meridian
Whirlpool Rapids
N.Y.C.R.R. Depot
Suspension Bridge
CLIFTON
Scale of Feet
Scale of One Mile
NIAGARA RIVER
C. S. R.R.
C.S.R.R. Depot
Clifton House
New Suspension Bridge
DRUMMONDSVILLE
NIAGARA FALLS
STATE OF NEW YORK
Prospect Park
American Falls
Luna Id.
Bird Id.
Bath Id.
Goat Island
Horse Shoe Falls
Sister Islands
Brother Id.
Cedar Island
N.Y.C.R.R. Depot
Erie R.R. Depot
Erie R.R.
N.Y.C.R.R.
PROVINCE OF ONTARIO
RAPIDS
C. S. R.R.
Chippewa Creek
MAP OF
NIAGARA FALLS!
From surveys executed in 1875, under the orders of Major C. B. COMSTOCK,
Corps of Engineers, Brevt. Brigadier General U S A.
DETROIT TO THE SEA.

A DAY AT NIAGARA.

ARRANGEMENTS have been made for checking hand bags at the depot, so that no one will be burdened during the day with the care of baggage. Little coupon tickets, good for carriage fare, for all day, from the depot, when train arrives in the morning, to the depot again when train leaves at 4 P. M., as well as for all tolls and admissions to places of interest about the Falls, will be for sale on the train by the manager of the excursion. A saving of about one-half in expense, saying nothing about profanity, can be secured by purchasing these coupon tickets. They are intended to be used where five persons will make a party and take a carriage together.

HORSE SHOE FALLS.

FOLLOW THE GUIDE-BOOK.

The recommendations of this guide in regard to using the coupon tickets at the Falls, should not be disregarded. Their use will save a great deal of trouble, time and expense It is also of importance that the party should not scatter, but should all go to the International for breakfast, as a special price has been obtained, which is conditional that they should provide for the entire excursion party.

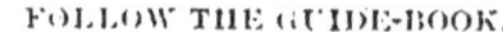

SEEING WITHOUT SUFFERING.

One of the greatest treats in store for patrons of this excursion is the provision made for a visit to Niagara Falls at the most enjoyable season of the year under the guidance of those who have been there so often as to be perfectly familiar with the best means of getting around and seeing the most in the least time with the greatest possible comfort

A description of Niagara Falls that did justice to the subject, or was satisfactory to the writer, probably has never been written; and surely the limit of these pages cannot be expected to contain one. The writer may write, the painter may paint, the orator may weave the magic spell of his eloquence, but it is all in vain when applied to Niagara. The very effort belittles the attempt It cannot be done. Niagara must be seen, and once seen it can never be forgotten.

For the edification of those who think of making the trip with us this year we have caused to be prepared a few excellent cuts, showing the "Horse Shoe Falls," the "American Falls," and a general view of the Falls from that inimitable coign of vantage near the track of the Canada Southern Railroad—the spot where the excursionists will get their first view of this stupendous exhibition of the Creator's might.

GENERAL VIEW OF NIAGARA FALLS FROM THE CANADA SOUTHERN R. R.

CORRECT MAP OF NIAGARA RIVER.

These are supplemented by an excellent outline map of the river and the surrounding places. It gives a better idea of the situation than any description could, and is mathematically correct, being a fac simile of the U. S Coast Survey map executed a few years ago under the orders of Gen. Comstock of the U. S. Engineers.

The EVENING NEWS excursion will arrive at Niagara at about 9 A. M. on the day after leaving Detroit. Will leave the cars at the Canada Southern depot immediately west of the Falls, and will find carriages awaiting to convey them across the river by the new suspension bridge to the International Hotel. After breakfast, if we choose to avail ourselves of the manager's carefully selected route, we will go to Prospect Park, which will include a ride down the inclined railroad to the foot of the American Falls, and after viewing the Falls from below, the line of march will be resumed toward Goat Island, where the grand panorama of rapids and falls will be brought to view. Next we will be driven to Whirlpool Rapids on the American side; thence back as far as the lower suspension bridge and across to Canada again and up the bank of the river, past the Horse Shoe Falls, to

AMERICAN FALLS.

the famous and wonderful Burning Springs. From this weird locality, with its suggestive blue lights fresh from the regions of the nether world, we will return, cross the river again at the upper or new suspension bridge for dinner at the International, and then, well paid for our visit to Niagara, and with the inner man well refreshed, we will return to the depot and wing our way toward the rising sun and the sea shore again.

Niagara is by no means the *highest* waterfall in the world, but it is beyond all peradventure the grandest and most sublime, as no other fall carries over it such an immense volume of water. Careful hydrographic measurements made by the most expert engineers in the employ of the government show that about 2,000,000 tons of water *per minute* go over the "American" and "Horse Shoe Falls," and if the reader of this little book desires to sentimentalize over what he imagines Niagara Falls to be like, the above figures will serve as a warp to be filled in by the magic weaving of his imagination.

STEAMER CHICORA.

LEAVING NIAGARA FALLS.

Resuming seats in the Canada Southern Railroad cars, a short run of about eighteen miles, and the shore of Lake Ontario, at the little old town of Niagara, is reached. Midway in this short ride a fine monument, 194 feet in height, will be noticed to the right (east), marking the spot where General Isaac Brock was killed, Oct. 13th, 1812, during the battle of Queenstown. It will be remembered that General Hull surrendered Detroit to General Brock on the 16th of August of the same year. The monument can be ascended by a spiral staircase inside.

NIAGARA

Is one of the oldest towns in Ontario and was formerly the capital of the Province. It is situated at the mouth of Niagara River (the Canada Southern cars will be exchanged at this point for the steamer Chicora).' Old Fort Niagara on the "American" (United States) side was captured from the French by the English, in 1759 and was the scene, also, of many conflicts between the whites and Indians.

STEAMER CHICORA.

The "bridge" upon which the excursion will cross Lake Ontario, has been especially prepared for this passenger route. She is 230 feet long and built of iron and steel in the strongest and most substantial manner for ocean service. And, as the hull is divided by iron bulkheads into five water-tight compartments—a precaution unusual in any lake steamers—strength and safety, the first requisites of a passenger steamer, are completely secured.

The steamer was built for, and did service as a blockade runner, and exhibits a little relic in the shape of the bell, now hanging in front of the wheel-house, upon which is to be read the former name of the *Chicora*, "Let Her B."

Supper will be served on board, on the "European plan." It is expected that plans for the sleepers on the Grand Trunk Railroad will be on board the steamer and that berths can be secured while crossing the lake.

LAKE ONTARIO

Is the smallest of the chain of the "Great Lakes," being 180 miles long by 35 miles wide, but is far from uninteresting, at least to the Indians, who gave it a name which means *beautiful*. It is not so subject to storms or change of temperature as the shallower lakes, on account of its great depth, the average being about 500 feet. The excursion will cross the lake from Niagara to Toronto in the afternoon of July 8th.

TORONTO.

The view of this city from the water is very fine indeed, and its buildings and wharves show to the best advantage. The landing will be at the depot of the Grand Trunk R. R.

Toronto was founded by Governor

CITY OF TORONTO.

Simcoe, in 1794, and was the capital of Upper Canada till 1841. Everything in it of importance, however, besides the name, which at that time was "York," was burned by United States troops in 1813. Its present population is about 70,000, and it ranks second in Canada in commercial importance. The finest hotel in this city is the QUEEN'S, which is first-class in all its appointments.

THE GRAND TRUNK R. R.

Is first reached by the excursion at Toronto. This road is in superb condition, having 1,053 miles of track laid with steel rails, and 337 with iron rails, upon which an army of workmen are constantly employed, so that it can never become seriously out of order.

The immense cost of building and maintaining the road may be inferred from the fact that Victoria Bridge at Montreal, representing but *two* of its *fourteen hundred miles*, cost over $7,000,000 in gold, to build, and costs a small fortune yearly to keep in repair.

The stock of the road is owned and controlled in England, but the general Canadian office is at Montreal.

The locomotives and passenger coaches are not excelled by any road in America, and, as all trains are run by telegraph, accidents seldom occur.

For summer pleasure travel this road is unexcelled, for it should be remembered that much of this route is as far north as Lake Superior, and equally as cool for summer travel. This road has four terminations, viz: Quebec, Portland, Buffalo and Detroit.

MAKING A NIGHT OF IT.

The seven hours' night ride of 161 miles from Toronto to Kingston will be spent in the traveler's "home"—a Pullman sleeper—in faithful imitation of the historical seven. The scenery that is *lost* during the night will be *found* again, when, on the return trip, this part of the route will be passed in the daytime.

KINGSTON

Is reached at about 3 A. M., but those occupying sleeping cars, will not be disturbed, as the cars will be backed down a side track and left standing near the dock until the arrival of the steamer from Toronto, which will stop long enough to take the excursion aboard, before resuming her course down the St. Lawrence River. Kingston is 392 miles from Detroit and 172 miles from Montreal which, latter place, could be reached, by those preferring to continue on the Grand Trunk Railroad, by 8 o'clock A. M. The tickets being good, for the railroad or steamer, at the holder's option.

The city of Kingston, which has a population of 15,000, was founded in 1672, by Governor DeCourcelles, receiving the name of Fort Cataraqui. Later, a massive stone fort was built by Count De-Frontenac, and received his name. In 1762 the place was taken by the British, who gave it its present name. As a place of defence it stands next in strength to Quebec. The batteries of Fort Henry are calculated for the reception of numerous cannon and mortars of the largest calibre. These, together with neighboring martello towers, form a formidable and efficient defense against any aggressive movement which might be directed against the city.

These fortifications are seen to excellent advantage from the steamer soon after it leaves the dock. The steamer which will be taken belongs to the

RICHELIEU & ONTARIO NAVIGATION CO.,

Who own eight passenger steamers upon the St Lawrence River. The company have their main office at 228 St. Paul st., Montreal. J. B Lamere is general manager, and Alex. Milloy, traffic manager. Six steamers, (the Corsican, Spartan, Corinthian, Passport, Algerian and Magnet) are engaged on the route between Toronto and Montreal. The other two steamers of this company alternate between Montreal and Quebec, being named after these two cities.

Breakfast and dinner will be served on board the steamer, tickets for which can be secured at the office of the purser on the lower deck for 50 cents each.

THE THOUSAND ISLANDS

Is the most numerous collection of river islands in the world. It commences a little above Kingston, and stretches down the river between 40 and 50 miles, for which distance the St. Lawrence is between 6 and 12 miles wide. Notwithstanding their name, the number of these islands far exceeds *a thousand;* there being

AT LEAST 1,500.

They lie partly in Canada, and partly within the bounds of the State of New York; the boundary line between the United States and Canada dividing them into about equal parts. Nowhere in the world is a more beautiful scene presented to the eye of the traveler than here. As the steamboat is piloted through the intricate channels, dodging here and there among the islands, showing each moment new and ever-varying beauties, the scene is

BEAUTIFUL BEYOND DESCRIPTION.

Islands of all sizes and shapes are scattered in profusion throughout the waters; some covered with vegetation, others bare and ragged rocks; some many acres in extent, others measuring but a few feet; some showing a bare, bald head, a little above the level of the water, while, a short distance off, a large island or rock, crowned with a considerable growth of pine or cedar will rise abruptly out of the water, to the height, probably, of 100 feet or more. These islands, too, have been the scene of

MOST EXCITING ROMANCE.

From their great number, and the labyrinth-like channels among them, they afforded an admirable retreat for the insurgents in the last Canadian insurrection' and for the American sympathizers with them, who, under the name of "patriots," sought to embarrass the British Government.

THE FIRST TOWN

On the right passed after leaving Kingston, is Clayton. This village is situated on the American side, opposite the "Thousand Islands," and was formerly of considerable importance as a lumber station. Opposite Clayton, on the Canadian side, is Gananoque, which is a flourishing town of about 3,000 inhabitants, and has become quite a favorite resort for tourists and pleasure seekers. The beauty of the islands and river, as seen from this point, cannot be surpassed.

ALEXANDRIA BAY

Is the next place to the right after leaving Clayton, and is romantic and highly picturesque. It is a place of resort for sportsmen. Some two or three miles below the village is a position from whence one hundred islands can be seen at one view. This place also is celebrated for its fishing and shooting. The beauty of the islands in this vicinity for several miles up and down the river can hardly be imagined without a personal visit. In the summer of 1872 President Grant and family and a party of their friends visited Alexandria Bay as the guests of Mr. Geo. M. Pullman, who owns one of the pleasantest islands of the group.

The large hotel at the head of the bay, to the right of the steamer, is the Thousand Island House, and just below it is the Crossman House.

BROCKVILLE

Is so named in honor of General Brock, who fell in battle at Queenstown Heights, in 1812. It might have appropriately been named *Rock*-ville, as its appearance makes plausible the statement, that here there are but two seasons of the year, eight months of ice and four months of rock. The excursion will pass during the *rock* season.

OGDENSBURG,

The next place of interest on the "American" side, was founded in 1748 by Abbe Francois Piquet but its fort, "La Presentation," was captured by the Mohawk Indians, in October, 1749. It has a population of 8 000 and is a beautiful and wealthy city, with wide streets and fine public buildings.

PRESCOTT

Is immediately opposite Ogdensburg, and connected with it by a steam ferry. It contains about 3,000 inhabitants, and previous to the opening of the Rideau Canal, was a place of importance in the carrying trade between Kingston and Montreal. A railroad has recently been built, which extends from Ottawa City to Prescott, and there connects the Ottawa River with the St. Lawrence.

WINDMILL POINT,

About a mile below Prescott, at a place called "Windmill Point," is a lighthouse, recently constructed from the stone of an old windmill, which for many years was one of the principal landmarks on the river. Its foundations are still to be seen. In the old building, in 1837, the rebels under Von Schulz, a Polish exile, established themselves, and were only dislodged after a most obstinate resistance, in which they suffered severe loss.

CHIMNEY ISLAND.

Six miles below Windmill Point, is Chimney Island, on which the remains of an old French fortification are to be seen.

GALLOP RAPIDS,

Which is about one mile below Chimney Island, is the first and smallest rapid on the river; in the phraseology of the "Phat boy," it is "a little one for a cent."

WADDINGTON

Is the next town on the American side; and in the river over against it is Ogden Island. On the Canada side is Morrisburg, formerly called West Williamsburg. It is called the Port of Morristown, and contains about two hundred inhabitants. A short distance below Morristown, on the Canada side, is Chrysler's Farm, where, in 1813 a battle was fought between the English and the Americans. The Americans were commanded by General Wilkinson, and were at that time descending the river to attack Montreal. The attempt was afterwards abandoned. Thirty miles below Ogdensburg is Louisville from whence stages run to Messena Springs, a popular summer resort, distant seven miles.

THE CANALS.

Passing Morrisburg, Aultsville and Farren's Point on the Canadian shore, we arrive at Dickinson's Landing, the head of the Cornwall canal. This canal, twelve miles in length, was built to avoid the Long Sault Rapids. The following is a statement of the various canals, the number of locks in each and their descent in feet:

NAMES.	Miles	Locks	L. Ft
Gallops Canal	2	2	8
Point Iroquois Canal	3	1	6
Rapid Platt Canal	4	2	11-6
Farren's Point Canal	¾	1	1
Cornwall Canal, Long Sault	11½	7	88
Beauharnois Canal, Coteau	.....	..	...
Cedars, Split Rock, Cascade Rapids	11¼	9	82-6
Lachine Canal, Lachine Rapids	8½	5	44-9
Fall on portions of the St. Lawrence between canals from Lake Ontario to Montreal			17
From Montreal to the tide water at Three Rivers	.....	.....	12-9
	41	27	2346

All of the passenger steamers and part of the freight craft "run" the rapids going *down*, but everything has to pass through the canals going up.

SHOOTING THE RAPIDS.

LONG SAULT RAPIDS,

The first of a remarkable series, which are almost continuous for a distance of nine miles, have an average velocity of 20 miles an hour. An island in the middle divides the rushing waters into two channels—the American channel and the "Lost" (Canadian) channel; a name given to it by the French boatmen, as they supposed that if a boat drifted into it, it would certainly be lost. Formerly the American or East Channel was mostly run by steamers, but of late the Lost Channel is mostly used. This channel presents a grand appearance, the water being lashed into a white foam for several miles. The passage on the southern channel is very narrow, and such is the velocity of the current, that a raft, it is said, will drift the nine miles in forty minutes. When a steamer enters within their influence, the steam is partly shut off and the engine slowed down to enable the pilot to keep her in the proper course, which is here very narrow. Great nerve, strength and skill are necessary to pilot the vessel, and several men are required at the wheel, and a tiller is attached to the rudder, itself, so that the tiller can be manned as well as the wheel. It requires four men at the wheel and two at the tiller to ensure safe steering. "One of the most singular sensations we experienced," says a distinguished traveler, "was that of sailing many miles perceptibly down hill." This going down hill by water produces a highly novel sensation, which is enhanced by the tremendous roar of the headlong, boiling current. The first passage of a steamer down these rapids was in 1840 This fall is comparatively described by the "phat boy" as being "*two* for a cent."

CORNWALL,

At the foot of Long Sault, on the Canada side, is a neat little town of about 5,000 inhabitants and contains some of the largest cotton and woolen mills in Canada.

ST. REGIS

Is an old Indian village, a little below Cornwall, on the south side of the river The tourist will observe from the deck of the steamer the old church, lifting its tin roof above the neighboring houses. The bell hanging in this church is associated with a deed of genuine Indian revenge. On its way from France it was captured by an English cruiser, and taken into Salem, Massachusetts, where it was sold to the church at Deerfield, in the same State. The Indians, hearing of the destination of their bell, set out for Deerfield, attacked the town, killed forty-seven of the inhabitants and took one hundred and twelve captives, "among whom was the pastor and his family." The bell was then taken down and conveyed to St. Regis, where it now hangs.

The boundary line between the United States and Canada passes near this village, and the course of the St. Lawrence is hereafter within Her Majesty's dominions.

LAKE ST. FRANCIS

Is the name of the expansion of the St. Lawrence which begins near Cornwall and St. Regis, and extends to Coteau du Lac, a distance of forty miles. The surface of this lake is interspersed with a great number of small islands. The village of Lancaster is situated on the northern side about midway of this lake.

COTEAU DU LAO

Is a small village, situated at the foot of Lake St. Francis. The name, as well as the style of the buildings, denotes its French origin.

COTEAU RAPIDS

Are just below Coteau du Lac, and fifty miles above Montreal. These rapids extend two miles.

CEDARS.

The village presents the same marks of French origin as Coteau du Lac. In the expedition of General Amherst, a detachment of three hundred men, that were sent to attack Montreal, were lost in the rapids near this place.

CEDAR RAPIDS

Commence seven miles below Coteau Rapids and near the village of Cedars. The passage through these rapids is very exciting. There is a peculiar motion of the vessel, which in descending seems like settling down as she glides from one ledge to another.

SPLIT ROCK RAPIDS

Immediately follow, in fact they are a continuation of the Cedar Rapids In passing the rapids of the Split Rock, a person unacquainted with the navigation of these rapids will almost involuntarily hold his breath until this ledge of rocks, which is distinctly seen from the deck of the steamer, is passed. The rocks do not rise above the water, and a passage 200 feet wide has been opened for the passage of steamers, by blasting.

CASCADE RAPIDS,

Which are entered soon after the passage of the former, terminate at the head of Lake St. Louis, where the dark waters of the Ottawa, by one of its mouths, join the St. Lawrence. These last three rapids in eleven miles have a descent of 82½ feet.

BEAUHARNOIS

Is a small village at the foot of the Cascades, on the south bank of the river. Here vessels, going up, enter the Beauharnois Canal, and pass around the rapids of the Cascades, Cedars and Coteau, into Lake St. Francis, a distance of fourteen miles. Mount Royal in the rear of Montreal, 30 miles distant, can be seen at this point.

LAKE ST. LOUIS.

Below the Cascades, and where the Ottawa river joins it from the north, the river again widens into a lake called St. Louis. In this lake is Nun's Island, which is beautifully cultivated, and belongs to the Grey Nunnery, at Montreal. There are many islands in the vicinity of Montreal belonging to the different nunneries, and from which they derive large revenues.

LACHINE

Is a small village at the foot of Lake St. Louis, nine miles from Montreal. It derived its name from the first settlers, who, when they reached this point, thought that they had discovered the passage which would lead them to China. The Lachine Rapids begin just below the village.

JEAN BAPTISTE, THE INDIAN PILOT.

CAUGHNAWAGA,

Lies on the south bank of the river near the entrance of the rapids. It is said that the Indians who had been converted by the Jesuits were called "Caughnawagas" or "praying Indians." Hence its name No one but Indians live in this village, which consists principally of one-story log houses. Just before reaching Caughnawaga, a canoe will be seen to emerge from the point of land on which the village is situated. The canoe contains Jean Baptiste, the famous pilot, and his two sons. The steamer stops her machinery and allows the canoe to come alongside and the pilot is taken aboard.

The Indian Pilot is an old grey-headed man of 60 odd years, but still possesses a splendid physique, and is "the lion of the hour." He wears a plaid shirt of bright colors and takes his post at the wheel, as oblivious to the notice he attracts as the most stolid of his race.

LACHINE RAPIDS

Are the last and most dangerous on the river, although the shortest, and are in sight of the city of Montreal. Before entering these rapids, the passengers are requested to sit or stand still in their places and to refrain from talking. The pilot and two assistants man the wheel and four men assist, in the steamer's stern, by handling the tiller. The steam is shut off, and as the steamer enters the rapids, nothing is heard but the sound of the waves as they dash themselves into a foam over the rocks. A ledge of rocks stretches across a portion of the channel, and for this the steamer is directly steered. When within a few yards of certain destruction the wheel is rapidly turned, and the boat, which an instant before seemed about to be dashed to pieces, glides gracefully past the reef amid the applause of the scores of passengers who crowd the forward deck. It is all intensely exhilarating. There is no occasion for fear of personal safety, as steamers have passed through the rapids every day of every summer for many years, and no lives have been lost.

VICTORIA BRIDGE.

The rapids all passed the steamer sails under one of the spans of the splendid Victoria bridge, surprising all the passengers that neither smoke-stack nor mast is carried away, so low does the bridge seem to the eye, from its great length of two miles. This bridge cost over $7,000,000 in gold.

The traveler now comes in full view of the city of Montreal, the most prominent object being the two towers of the church Notre Dame.

VICTORIA BRIDGE, MONTREAL.

MONTREAL.

ON arriving at Montreal, the steamer will enter the lock at the mouth of the Lachine Canal, and the gates being closed and the water let in underneath the steamer, the deck of the steamer will soon rise to a level with the dock. A mob of hackmen will do the honors of your reception, and in the absence of sufficient police regulation the tourist is compelled to make quick and arbitrary selection of the hack or carriage desired. Special rates have been arranged for the excursion at the Windsor hotel, which is one of the finest hotels on the continent. A suite of rooms will be thrown open free of charge, for toilet purposes, and a sumptuous repast in the finest dining room in America will be in readiness Plans of the sleeping cars will be at the railroad ticket office in the hotel rotunda, where those desiring such accommodations should secure them.

The train will start for the mountains at 9:45 P. M. The Windsor Hotel is about a mile from the steamer landing, and about half a mile from the Grand Trunk railroad depot.

FOR MORE THAN TWO HUNDRED YEARS

Montreal, in all her superbness of situation for commerce and manufactures, languished as an outpost of Quebec. Founded by M. de Maissonenne in 1649 (though "Hochelaga" had been discovered in 1535), and first named Ville Marie, Marystown, or Marysville as a modern translation would make it. It is one of the oldest cities on the continent, and by the indomitable push and enterprise of its citizens has been made one of the most important.

Montreal takes its name from the magnificent mountain hump at whose base it stands. The city is situated upon an island of the same name, at the juncture of the dark Ottawa with the St. Lawrence, and its railroad communication with the world is obtained by the Victoria bridge, the bridge at St. Anne's (both belonging to the Grand Trunk railway), and the bridges to the northwest, of the Montreal and Occidental railway. Of the Victoria bridge fuller mention will be made later. The population is estimated at 180,000, but if the suburbs of Hochelaga, St. Jean Baptiste village, St. Henri and St. Cunegorde be counted in, it would probably reach to nearly a quarter of a million. Of this population three-fifths are French Canadian, and the remainder of English, Irish and Scotch descent. It is calculated that there are 30,000 Irish Catholics in Montreal.

The tourist, on reaching the city, will be struck, first of all, with the apparently endless line of

MASSIVE STONE DOCKS.

This mighty work, extending for mile after mile along the river front, from the colossal outlet of the Lachine Canal to Hochelaga, was undertaken when the maritime importance of the port was in its infancy; and it was an investment which has repaid itself many thousands of times. Before the revetment wall was built, the city was exposed yearly to inundation on the break-up of the ice in the spring; the wall now forms a barrier, while the dock system, as a whole, is the most magnificent on the continent, and surpassed by but two or three others on the globe. Whole fleets of ocean steamships, arrive, discharge and load here every year, as do sailing vessels without number. Montreal obtained this great commerce by the energy of her citizens, who went to work and dug a channel through the flats of Lake St. Peter. Forty years ago it was a dangerous thing for ships of 300 tons to move up to Montreal. Now steamships of 4,000 tons steam up and down the channel almost every day in the week.

The docks, the first mark of Montreal's forward movement, are indicative of the character of the modern city. Everything is on a large and generous scale. The old French streets near the river, which till 1832 sufficed for all the purposes of trade and residence, have been abandoned to trade; some as they stood a century ago, but others after having been pulled down and two or three run into one. Commerce has laid its hand upon territory once sacred to the church, convents and such like, and paid terrific tribute to the religious communities owning the land. For the site of Montreal, and in fact all the land on the island, is the property of the Seminary of St. Sulpice. The land was granted the seminary by the King of France, and not a foot has the seminary let go except upon the church's own terms —never unfavorable to the church. Outside of this the church owns, it is estimated, $12,000,000 worth of property within the corporate limits of Montreal.

Ascending from the steamboat landing and going a short distance up town, we find ourselves upon a spacious avenue known as

JACQUES CARTIER SQUARE,

Which brings us at once to the heart of the city. The famous Notre Dame street runs at right angles with the square, at whose upper end is a monument to Lord Nelson. The great sea-dog is represented in colossal form on the top of a Tuscan column When the monument was erected in 1804 it was considered a marvel of art, but a different opinion is entertained nowadays.

To the right we have the new city hall, a splendid structure recently completed at immense cost. It is built of gray Montreal stone, a hard, durable material, not easily worked, but presenting a fine appearance. A good deal remains to be done before the hall and its grounds may be regarded as fulfilling the dreams of the projectors of both. Immediately opposite is the Normal school, under the charge of the Roman Catholic clergy. This building is probably the most ancient in Montreal. It was in the olden times the house of the governors, and possesses much interest to the antiquarian. Embowered in trees, the Court house, a stately edifice built upon a severely classical model, uplifts its majestic portico. This hall of justice occupies the site of the old jail of Montreal, and has been a costly investment to suitors ever since its erection, for upon every civil action is taxed a sum to be applied to the court house fund. The rear of the court house faces upon the Champ de Mars (Campus Martius), or parade ground for the troops. It is a splendid elevated plain upon which 2,500 troops might be nicely maneuvred, and have been, many a time, during British occupation. The Champ de Mars formed a portion of the fortifications of Montreal, constructed in 1758, and torn down within the memory of many of the present generation. It is still a favorite drill ground. Slipping away from this martial ground we pass St. Gabriel's church, a queer old structure, the oldest Presbyterian church in Canada, erected shortly after the conquest, and numbering among its congregation to-day descendants of its founders. Across the way are the Montreal offices of the local government.

Regaining Notre Dame street, we are enabled to peer into some of the old French thoroughfares, St. Vincent street, for instance. Here everything is ancient and time-stained. The roadway is only about half as wide as an average Detroit alley, the sidewalks, a modern improvement, about a yard, perhaps less, in width. The houses are old, black, frowsy and forbidding. Here you have on one side (on St. Jean Baptiste street) a blind wall; the old wall of a convent which formerly absorbed the best part of the town; here, you have a lot of houses whose overhanging roofs threaten to tumble upon you, and from whose cobwebby windows come whiffs of the odors of a by-gone century. Nearly opposite a broad descending avenue leading to St. Lawrence Main street, a great artery of retail trade, is the gateway leading to the chapel of the Nuns of the Congregation of Notre Dame. The good ladies had the sense to see that trade was coming their way, and accordly built up the front of their property into handsome stores which now yield splendid rents. To the right, a little further down, is a splendid range of stores, known as the "Cathedral Block," from being erected on the site of the Anglican cathedral, burned down in 1834. A few steps now bring us to the Place d' Armes, an exquisite little park serving as a breathing place in a quadrangle of palaces. First you have, looming 221 feet in the air above you, the massive towers of the parish

CHURCH OF NOTRE DAME,

An immense structure with accommodation for 8,000 worshipers easily, and 12,000 at a pinch. It was commenced in 1824, and has been building more or less ever since, for it is not yet finished, and no one knows when it will be. The interior has just undergone a gorgeous process of painting in the Byzantine style. Every inch of the edifice has been hand-painted in countless designs, at immense cost. The decorations of the church are superb, and a statue of the Virgin to the right of the grand altar, will well repay inspection. Vastness is the characteristic of this fane in every respect. In the western towers of the "Paroisse," (Parwasse) as the French call the church, is hung the largest bell on the continent, the "Gros Bourdon." This monster, weighing over ten tons, has a mouth so capacious that 30 men might stand under it, and it requires the strength of 16 men to ring it. Visitors are admitted to the tower, and may have the pleasure of tramping up several hundred steps for 25 cents. The reward is worth all the trouble, for the view from the platform at the top is superb. In the eastern tower there is a splendid chime of bells, but as French Canadians can never be taught to chime, they are always swung, and owing to the number of occasions upon which bells are found necessary in the Roman ritual, they are seldom silent.

THE SEMINARY OF ST. SULPICE

Adjoins the Parish Church. On its front is a queer old clock which rings the hours, halves and quarters. The old gate of the seminary still remains with the monogram A. M. (Ave Maria) over it, but the glory of the place has departed, so far as the work of the seminary is concerned, to the "priests' farm" or Monklands, where the college is now located. The land was too valuable to keep for college purposes, and so was sold off, until little now remains but the church, the presbytery, and the seminary gardens. Turning into the Place D'Armes again we find facing us the really splendid portico of the Bank of Montreal. The entablature of this structure is a work of art of uncommon merit. The bank has the largest paid up capital, $12,000,000, of any on the continent. Adjoining it to the right, is the People's Bank, diagonally across the way, the Jacques

Cartier Bank, a rather unfortunate French Canadian institution; on St. James Street the Banque du Peuple, a conservative, safe, French concern. Besides these, in handsome structures, are the Metropolitan, City and District, Ontario, Toronto, Cosmopolitan Exchange, and Union banks. Molson's and the Merchants' banks are stone structures which will command particular attention from their architectural beauty and evident costliness. The Merchants' bank is the creation of Sir Hugh Allen, Canada's steamship king, and has a paid up capital of $9,000,00C.

We are now upon great St. James Street, for its whole length remarkable for imposing and magnificent structures, chief among which is the Post Office, recently completed by the Canadian government.

At the corner of St. James and St. Peter Streets, and opposite the Merchants' bank, is the hall of the Mechanics' Institute, a handsome, substantial building, which was for many years Montreal's only concert room, or available hall for any purpose. It has a fine library and reading room, and in many ways the Institute influences for good the rising generation of Montreal. A few steps will bring us to Victoria Square, a splendid row of buildings, the "Albert Block," so named in honor of the late Prince Consort, furnishes a lordly abiding place for the chief officers and staff of the

GRAND TRUNK RAILWAY.

The broad street running at right angles to the river here is McGill Street, and it is lined with great stone ware houses of elegant architecture. It is the centre of the wholesale dry goods and clothing trade.

In Victoria Square, a very handsome park, is a statue of Queen Victoria, by Marshall Wood, who had the cheek to charge the city $10 000 for a lump of bronze which is as much unlike the queen as Vinnie Ream's statue is unlike Lincoln.

Victoria Square was, in 1877, the scene of the Orange riot. The unfortunate young man, Hackett, was murdered on the east side of the square at the door of a large wholesale dry goods store, in which he tried to obtain shelter when chased by a blood-thirsty mob,but from which he was shamefully repulsed. Victoria Square practically divides the business part of Montreal from "Griffintown," the quarter most inhabited by the opponents of Orangeism. To the left, as we cross Craig Street, we find the superb building of the Young Men's Christian Association. The Y. M. C. A. of Montreal is the

PARENT SOCIETY OF THE WORLD,

Having been founded in 1551, It is now housed in a Gothic building which cost $50,000, has a fine library and reading-room, and an elegant lecture hall (Association Hall) for lecture purposes and services. The work, in different departments carried on by the association, is very extensive, necessitating a large expenditure of money and great personal sacrifice on the part of the active members.

Leaving the hall and passing along Radegonde street, we arrive at the foot of

BEAVER HALL

Hill, so called because the Hudson Bay Company in the good old fur trading days had their headquarters here. Those were the days when everything was estimated by its relation to the value of a beaver skin. There are some, however, who call it Piety Hill, from the churches marking its ascent. First we have Zion church, Congregational, then the church of the Messiah, Unitarian, looking considerably, in some respects, like the bartizan of a mediæval castle. Across the street is the First Baptist church, and opposite it St. Andrew's, built on the model of Salisbury Cathedral. As we move along in this district we begin to understand why Montreal has been called a city of churches, for one is met at almost every step. Thus, as you go along Dorchester street, after you pass to the right the coldly palatial quarters of the St. James Club, you are face to face with St. Paul's church, (Presbyterian) a fine specimen of the decorated Gothic, where Rev. John Jenkins, father of the celebrated author of

"GINX'S BABY"

Preaches to an aristocratic congregation. In a vast square, contiguous to St. Paul's is in process of erection a temple which will be, when completed, one of the wonders of the continent. It is the Cathedral of St. Peter, and it is being built on the model of St. Peter's at Rome,but one fourth smaller. Though eight years have been spent upon what has thus far been accomplished, little, comparatively speaking, has been done, and it is not probable that the present generation of the faithful will ever attend mass within the precincts of St. Peter's. The church, which will cost no one knows how much, is being built by the voluntary contributions of the people.

We are now at Dominion Square, and before us looms up the Windsor,

CANADA'S ROYAL HOTEL,

Where the EVENING NEWS excursionists will find elegant quarters during their stay in Montreal. The Windsor Hotel grew out of the enterprise of a number of gentlemen headed by Sir Hugh Allan who were dissatisfied with the hotel accommodation of the city. Taking the Palmer house, Chicago, as their model, they went to work and spent over a million in a hotel which may have one or two equals, but certainly no superiors on the continent. The lessee of the hotel, Mr. Worthington, pays as rent 4 per cent. on $1,000,000, or $40,000 per annum. The furniture, carpets, etc., he put in himself. The excursionists will be better able to judge of its magnificence after they have had some experience of its hospitality.

The excursionist who will ascend the cupola will enjoy a splendid view of the river, spanned by the mighty Victoria bridge. He will see countless spires rising around him. Opposite the hotel, to continue the naration as to churches, are the Primitive Methodist, American Presbyterian and Methodist Episcopal; opposite the park but a little distance down is St. George's church, (Episcopal), a dainty specimen of Gothic; to the left can be seen Erskine church (Presbyterian), and the slender stone spire of Christ church. Christ church deserves special mention, though every one of the churches named are handsome and costly stone edifices. It is one of the finest churches on the continent, and the cathedral of the primate of Canada. It is built of Montreal limestone, principally, with dressings of Caen stone, imported from France. Elaborate sculpturing lavishly displayed, marks the exterior, while the interior is a mass of rich, yet harmonious and artistic decoration. The chief feature of attraction is a spire of solid masonry, rising some 200 feet, a piece of bold and able stone craft In the cathedral close is a superb memorial cross to perpetuate the name of the late Bishop Fulford. The palace of the Metropolitan or Senior Bishop of Canada, is also on the grounds To the west of the palace is Synod Hall, better known to most Montrealers as "Breach of Promise Hall." And for this reason: There was a

BRIDAL CHAMBER, WINDSOR HOTEL.

LADY OF SPUNK

Who was wooed by a merchant with much wealth. He was fickle, jilted her and married another lady who had but a short time before told the man she loved that she could not afford to marry poverty. The young lady of spunk sued her umquwhile and faithless lover for breach of promise, and got a heavy verdict. With the damages she built Synod Hall, for a church school, disdaining to use a penny of the money for herself. Mark what further befel the faithless lover. He died two years after his marriage, and his widow, enriched by his fortune, married the lover whose poverty once had been a barrier.

More time might be devoted to churches, but we must close with a visit to the church of the Gesu or Jesuit's church on Bleury Street. The Jesuits in spite of all attempts to prevent them regaining foothold in Canada, have succeeded in recovering the ground they lost at the Conquest, and have now practically regained control over Catholic education in Lower Canada. Whatever may be the commonly received opinion of Jesuitism, one thing is certain of its teaching. it tends toward making men good citizens. Their church in Montreal is famous for its frescos, executed by a great Italian artist The fane is, to express much in a few words, a veritable art gallery, in which hours may be spent in the study of grand conceptions. Exquisite music is a feature of the services in the Gesu. Controversial sermons are preached every Sunday night, and the hours are so timed that the Protestants, returning from the services in their own churches, and who drop into the Gesu to hear the music, get the benefit of skillful attacks upon every form of faith which conflicts with that of Rome.

There are in all some 80 churches in Montreal and numerous missions. The church property, Catholic and Protestant, is estimated at $20,000,000

Leaving the Windsor, for an afternoon's drive, the most enjoyable use of time to be made is a progress to Mount Royal Park. This mountain furnishes Montreal, in the language of Lord Dufferin, the

FINEST PARK IN THE WORLD.

A whole mountain is taken up with the breathing and enjoying place of a people. From a field, broken up with gentle ascents, a road winding by ways which present beauty at every turn, has been cut and made so that a hill, once only accessible to the stoutest and most indomitable climber, is now easily reached to its summit by a carriage and pair. The roadway is superb, and when the summit is reached, what a vision! There stretches away the dreamy length of the St. Lawrence, islanded as far as the eye can reach. The Catskills are in the distance, and the tips of the Green Mountains. Nearer are the humps of Montarville and Belœil, while to the north may be seen rising the blue hills of the Laurentides. The city lies at the foot, humming with busy industry. Near by, hewn out of the eternal rock, are the immense reservoirs from which Montreal draws her daily 40,000,000 gallons of water, and from here all her institutes of learning are visible. There, for instance, at the base of the mountain, is McGill University, famous throughout the world, through its principal, Dr. Dawson, the great scientist, who has devoted his life to the advocacy of God in science. The University is the centre of Canadian thought and progress. It is situated in the midst of magnificent grounds, and around it cluster the homes of some of the grandest men in Canada. The Presbyterian Theological College occupies a picturesque position upon the breast of the hill.

From the mountain we see the long streets of palatial homes which the Montreal merchants have made for themselves. Montreal, like Detroit, is a city of homes. The residental quarters are replete with the elegant nests of successful families. Sherbrooke street, St. Catherine street, McGill College avenue, and a dozen other such like avenues, open themselves out, bud-like, into a host of splendid homes. The most magnificent of all may need a mention specially, and that is "Ravenscrag," the seat of Sir Hugh Allan. This castle, it is nothing less, has several times been the abode of royalty. It is a baronial residence, covering a large expanse.

The drive around the mountain is about nine miles long, and will take you over a good deal of historic ground. It will take you past the Mount Royal Cemetery, one of the most splendid cities of the dead in the world, and the Cote des Neiges Cemetery, where lie, under a pompous monument, the bones of those whom the Brtish government found necessary to hang after the rebellion of 1837. These cemeteries lie in gentle, silent valleys between the mountains, where there is never sound of human strife.

Montreal is on the whole, a great, strong city, in manufactures, in commerce and in navigation. She is the great distributing centre of Canada. Here is where the great Allan Line of steamers turn out their enormous freights. Here the Grand Trunk centres its business. Here the grain trade of the west turns its yellow wealth into the elevators. Here the fur trade of the north looks for its return in corn and kind. Here is done the great clothing, boot and shoeing trade of the country. The metal works, wood works, car works, drug works, in fact nearly all the works of the country centre here. The warehouses of Montreal, on the great business streets are unsurpassed in magnificence of architecture in the world, and the city as a whole, is one well worthy of the study of every man who wishes to see how large a growth may be effected from small and well directed efforts.

The Victoria bridge is a work undertaken by the Grand Trunk railway company of Canada. It connects Pointe St. Charles with the Southern shore, but would never have been necessary had the managers of the Grand Trunk had the common sense to see that their interest lay in building up the well cultivated North Shore. The bridge is 90 feet short of being two miles long. It is a tubular bridge, resting upon 24 piers, so built as to resist the pressure of ice, the centre pier being 156 feet in height to permit the passage of steamers; the cost was some $8,000,000, and the loss of life during its construction, was considerable. It was designed by the great Stephenson and carried to a completion by Sir Morton Peto. As a bridge it has no equal in the world, but science has proved, since the Prince of Wales drove the last rivet in 1860, that long bridges can be put up at a much cheaper rate. A project is now on foot to bridge the river at about one-twelfth of what it cost to build the Victoria.

A CHANGE OF COUNTRIES.

DURING the third night of the excursion tour, Her Majesty's Dominions will be exchanged for the territory of the old Green Mountain State, the exact place of transfer being at Norton Mills, which is 132 miles from Montreal, and 76 miles from Gorham, N. H., which will be the stopping place at the White Mountains. It is also but sixteen miles to Island Pond, where a stop of one hour will be made for breakfast. The custom-house officers, at this place, examine all baggage checked *from Canada*. Note the distinction: Baggage checked at Detroit to Gorham or Portland, will go through Canada without stoppage or examination; but anything taken from Canada to the United States, or *vice versa*, will be stopped and examined at the boundary. If it is merely passing from Detroit to Gorham or Portland without stoppage, it will need no attention; but if it started from any place in Canada, then it will be removed from the baggage car to the examining room, where it will remain until the owner unlocks it and permits examination by the collector of customs.

THE BAGGAGE WILL BE LEFT

At the station, in such a case, unless the owner attends to it. It will be the same also on returning from Portland, when *en route* to Quebec.

ISLAND POND,

So named from being situated upon the banks of a mountain lake, three and a half miles long by one mile wide, is a village of 1,200 inhabitants, and is 1,300 feet above the level of the sea. Three miles from the station Mt. Bluff rises 1,200 feet high, and affords from its summit a magnificent view. A steam yacht on the lake, with abundant facilities for fishing, might be mentioned as among the means of enjoyment at this place.

THE TWO FINE HOTELS

At this place are under one management, and will have a breakfast in waiting for the hungry excursionists. They are respectively, the Island Pond House and the Stewart House, and are admirably conducted.

THE OLD GRANITE STATE.

The New Hampshire boundary will be passed at North Stratford, 15 miles southeast of Island Pond. The river which is crossed at this place is the Connecticut. Traveling 11 miles nearly south

GROVETON JUNCTION

Is reached at about 8 A. M., July 10th. Those who desire to attend the American Institute of Instruction should change cars, and take the road that runs south on the *west* side of the White Mountains. The manager will have side trip tickets (for sale after leaving Montreal) from Groveton Junction, around to the Fabyan House, (where the Institute is to be held July 8, 9, 10 and 11) thence to the summit of Mt. Washington by the elevated railroad. Carriages will be in waiting at the summit for those who have taken this side trip, and will convey them to the Glen House on the east side, where they will rejoin the excursion. Full information, prices, etc., will be given in ample time after leaving Montreal.

By taking this side trip, teachers can attend the

LAST TWO DAYS OF THE INSTITUTE,

Or, what may be still better, the next to the last (and best) day of the Institute (the 10th) can be attended, and by taking the afternoon train up the mountain, the night can be spent on the summit and the descent by carriages made the following day.

Returning to the general excursion route, via the Grand Trunk Railroad, the next station after leaving Groveton Junction is

GROVETON.

After which the railroad crosses the Ammonoosuc river, with Cape Horn and Mt. Bellamy on the right, and Percy Peaks and Bowback Mountains on the left front and left. Portions also of the Stratford and Sugar-Loaf Mountains are seen to the north; and on the other side the Pilot Mountains soon swing into view. As the train speeds to the east, the south peak of the Percies advances over the higher north peak, and finally eclipses it. The line leaves the river for about 4 miles, and runs under the Pilot Mountains, then crosses the river and stops at

STARK WATER,

Which is picturesquely situated, with the precipice of the Devil's Slide on the left, and Mill Mountain close at hand on the right. The former is a sheer cliff 5,000 feet high, and bears evidence of ancient natural convulsions. Mill Mountain is 2,000 feet high, and is sometimes ascended from Stark by a walk of 1½ miles through the woods. Beyond Starkwater station fine views are given on the right and in retrospect, including the Pilot and Crescent Ranges, the Percy Peaks, and Green's Ledge, sharply cut off on the south.

WEST MILAN.

Just before and after leaving the station at West Milan the traveler who looks forward from the right side of the train gains a beautiful distant view of the Presidential Range, which is arranged in stately order. The line now leaves the banks of the rapid Ammonoosuc, and follows the course of Dead River through a dull and uninteresting country.

At the lonely water station of Milan between West Milan and Berlin Falls, the track is 1080 feet above the sea. Head Pond is soon passed, on the right, and the traveler gains frequent glimpses of the White Mountains on the right. The train soon crosses to the course of another Dead River, passes a small pond, and approaches Berlin Falls

BERLIN FALLS,

The last stopping place before Gorham is of little interest apart from its natural surroundings. On the left, over the diverging track of the Berlin Lumber Company, the far away blue peak of Goose Eye is seen; the fine cliffs of Mt. Forest are passed just before arriving at the station.

Between Berlin Falls and Gorham there is a high descending grade, the track falling at the rate of 50 feet to the mile. Occasional glimpses of the Androscoggin River are gained, and on either side are mountain-ranges.

GORHAM,

Which is 772 miles from Detroit by the route traveled, 208 miles from Montreal, and 91 miles from Portland, is a place of about 1,000 permanent population, on the Androscoggin River. In the summer months, however, the tourists gather here from every point of the compass and the place is lively and interesting. In its proximity to the mountains consists its sole attraction, although Mt. Washington cannot be seen until the party arrives at or near the Glen House. The large hotel at the left, is the Alpine House, owned by W. & C. R. Milliken, the proprietors of the Glen House, which is eight miles away up in the mountains. Here the cars are exchanged for coaches, and the railroad for the mountain road which follows up the banks of the

PEABODY RIVER

To the Glen. The road from Gorham to the Glen crosses and recrosses this little river, which, after heavy rains, or in the spring when the snow melts on the mountains, is a noisy, rushing mountain torrent. The river is filled and environed with huge masses of rocks, with which nature has produced many picturesque effects.

THE GLEN HOUSE

Is situated at the immediate base of the Mt. Washington (or Presidential) range, and the view from the piazza of the hotel is one of the finest in the mountains. The sharp pointed peak directly in front of the hotel is Mt. Adams, 5,794 feet high—to the left is what appears to be a triple pointed mountain, but which, in reality, consists of three peaks, the first being Mt. Jefferson, 5,714 feet high, next Mt. Clay, 5,552 high, and farthest to the left is Mt. Washington, which although apparently a lesser peak, is really 6,293 feet high, being the loftiest of them all. The distance to the summit of Mt. Washington from the Glen House, is eight miles, and the carriage road lies over Mts. Jefferson and Clay.

The summits of these peaks are frequently capped in the clouds, which gives a better idea of the height than any guide book statistics can possibly do. The Glen House is most favorably located of all the hotels in the mountains to obtain views of this range—the house itself is one of the largest in the United States, and is lighted with gas, and has every modern improvement. The proprietors Messrs. W. & C. R Milliken, are thorough hotel men, and their success is the best evidence that they thoroughly understand how to cater to the wants of the traveling public. The excursion party will spend two days at the Glen House, which will give ample time to ascend Mt. Washington, visit Glen Ellis and Crystal Cascade Falls, with a margin left for fishing for brook trout in the Peabody River, or strolling *ad libitum*. Not the least of the attractions at the Glen House is the table, at which the tourist is generally a most devoted and appreciative attendant. The fare is unexcelled and the service is a novelty in dining room management, for the waiters are all college students who spend their vacations in recuperating at the mountains and at the same time replenishing their depleted purses.

THE WHITE MOUNTAINS

CONSIST of more than 200 peaks that cover an area of 2,700 miles. · They are naturally divided into two divisions by the Saco river, each side being again sub-divided on the east by the Peabody and Ellis rivers, and on the west by the Pemigewasset River. Topographically considered, the mountains are grouped into nine sub-divisions, viz:

1. The Starr-King group.
2. The Mt. Carter group.
3. The Mt. Washington range,
4. The Cherry Mt. District.
5. The Mt. Willey range.
6. The Carrigan group.
7. The Passaconaway range.
8. The Twin Mt. group.
9. The Profile Mt. group.

THE SCENERY

Of the White Mountains compares favorably with the Swiss Alps, and those who have traveled widely in foreign lands are generally most enthusiastic in speaking of their grandeur and beauty. Those who have simply *passed by* the mountains on the railroad, are not qualified to judge of the scenery, except in the most superficial manner.

The tourist needs to stop a day or two at least, when, exchanging the Pullman for the mountain coach, the very heart of the mountains should be penetrated. Fine as are some of the views that are to be gleaned from the windows or rear platform of the train on the Grand Trunk railway, *they do not compare*, in scarcely any sense of the word, with that obtained from the veranda of the Glen House, and that in turn becomes weak and insipid as the tourist stands, a mile and a quarter higher, among or rather *above* the clouds, on the summit of Mt. Washington. The *summits* only of some of the loftiest peaks escaped the tremendous smoothing and "polishing off" that the rest received during the ice period, which accounts for the flowing instead of acute outlines. Mt. Adams, which is a sharply defined peak, is a marked exception, however.

The forty-five names given below are those by which the

PRINCIPAL PEAKS

Are now known. The figures attached give the height in feet.

Adams	5 791	Lincoln	5,100
Anderson	4,000	Moriah	4,653
Bald	3,978	Madison	5,365
Baldface	3,600	Monroe	5,384
Black	3,571	Moat	3,200
Carter	4,702	North Twin	5,000
Carter Dome	4,830	Osceola	4,400
Clay	5 552	Pleasant	4,764
Clinton	4,320	Profile	1,200
Cherry	3,670	Paugus	2,829
Carrigan	4,678	Passaconaway	4,200
Chocorua	3,540	Starr-King	3,800
Campton	1,742	South Twin	5,094
Doublehead	3,120	Sandwich Dome	4,000
Franklin	4,904	Tom	3,200
Field	4,070	Table	3,781
Hayes	2 917	Tecumseh	4,000
Hale	2,337	Tripyramid	3,542
Haystack	2,787	Wildcat	4,350
Hancock	4,420	Washington	6,293
Jefferson	5,714	Willey	4,330
Kancamagus	1,523	Whiteface	4,007
Lafayette	5,259		

IN THE HEART OF THE MOUNTAINS.

MT. WASHINGTON which is 6,293 feet, or nearly a mile and a quarter high, rises over 500 feet above the loftiest of the surrounding peaks. On account of this elevation, the summit forms an arctic island in the temperate zone, having the same climate as Greenland at 70° north latitude. This is shown both by the temperature and the vegetation. The latitude is 44° 16′ 25″ north, and the longitude is 76° 16′ 25″ west. The interest in this mountain is enhanced by knowing that the highest geological authorities place it among the very earliest formations of the earth's surface. Isaac Hill says: "Mt. Washington had been thousands of years in existence before the internal fires upheaved the Alps."

PROOFS OF THE ICE PERIOD.

The grooves and scratches on all but the south side show the course of the ice-bearing ocean of the glacial epoch. These marks are found to within 1,100 feet of the summit, hence the surrounding valleys must have been filled with ice, a mile thick, which, slowly moving south, finally submitted to a southern sun. Another proof that Mt. Washington affords of the ice period, and which makes it of great interest to the scientist, is a recent discovery that a flying insect found on

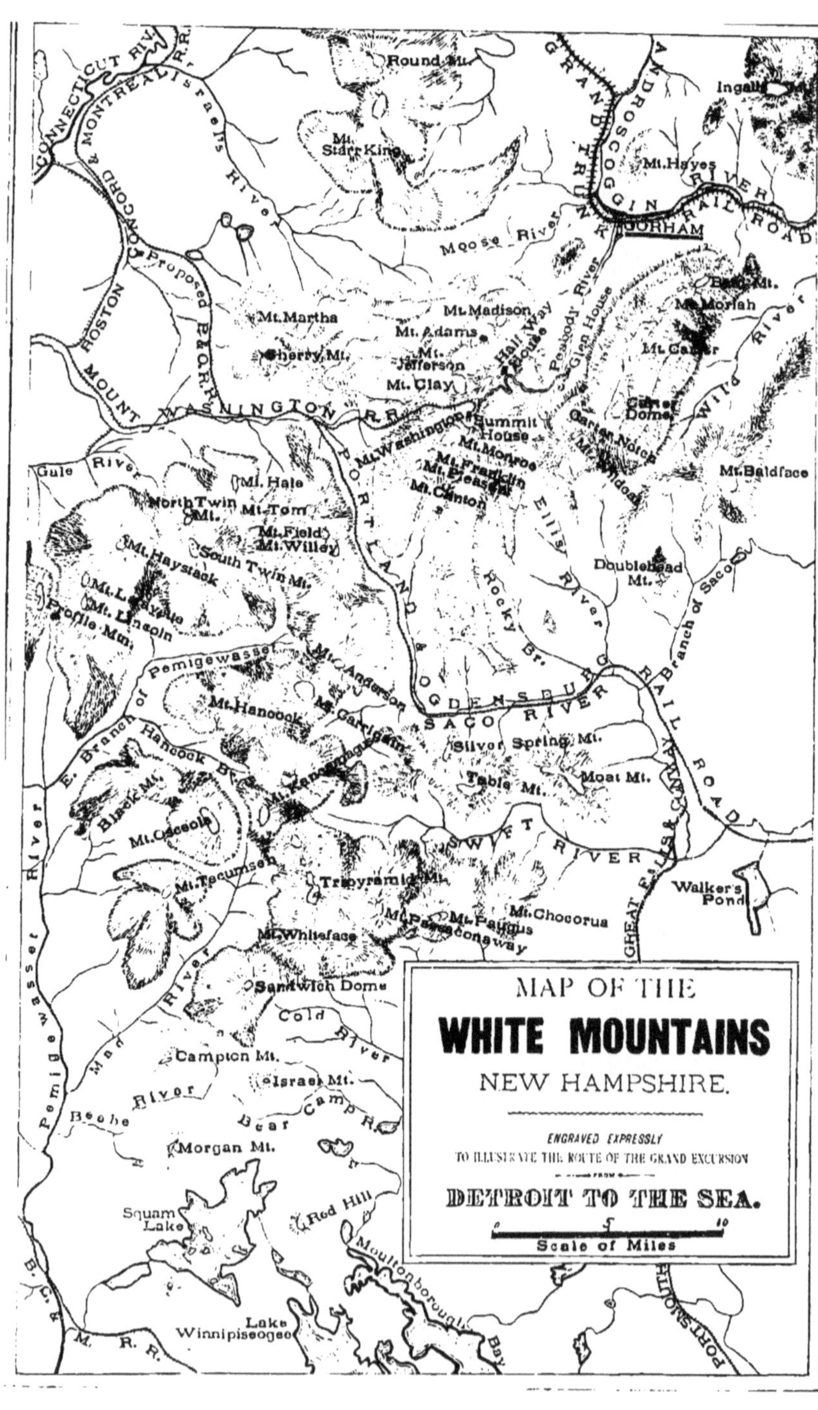
MAP OF THE
WHITE MOUNTAINS
NEW HAMPSHIRE.
ENGRAVED EXPRESSLY
TO ILLUSTRATE THE ROUTE OF THE GRAND EXCURSION
FROM
DETROIT TO THE SEA.
Scale of Miles
Round Mt.
Mt. Starr King
Mt. Hayes
GORHAM
Moose River
Mt. Martha
Mt. Madison
Mt. Adams
Mt. Jefferson
Mt. Clay
Summit House
Mt. Monroe
Carter Notch
Mt. Baldface
Gale River
Mt. Hale
Mt. Tom
Mt. Field
Mt. Willey
South Twin Mt.
Mt. Haystack
Profile Mtn.
Doublehead Mt.
Ellis River
Rocky Br.
Pemigewasset
Mt. Anderson
Mt. Hancock
Mt. Carrigain
SACO RIVER
Silver Spring Mt.
Table Mt.
Moat Mt.
Hancock Br.
Black Mt.
Mt. Osceola
SWIFT RIVER
Mt. Tecumseh
Tripyramid Mt.
Mt. Chocorua
Mt. Paugus
Mt. Passaconaway
Mt. Whiteface
Walker's Pond
Sandwich Dome
Cold River
Campton Mt.
Israel Mt.
Mad River
Beebe River
Bear Camp R.
Morgan Mt.
Red Hill
Squam Lake
Lake Winnipiseogee
Moultonborough Bay
M. R. R.
MOUNT WASHINGTON R.R.
GRAND TRUNK
ANDROSCOGGIN RIVER
PORTLAND & OGDENSBURG RAIL ROAD
GREAT FALLS & CONWAY
Wild River
Branch of Saco
Pemigewasset River
CONNECTICUT RIV.
BOSTON CONCORD & MONTREAL R.R.
Proposed

the summit, but no where else in the United States, is the same as others known to be native only in latitudes north of 70°. The theory is, that they accompanied the ice south as far as Mt. Washington, and by the melting away of the ice with which it was surrounded, were finally stranded on the summit, where they still find a congenial climate.

VEGETATION.

Not only is the *fauna* of the frigid zone found, but, as is well known, the *flora* of Mt. Washington is identical with that of the Arctic regions. He who ascends to this altitude has a similar opportunity for botanic study, as if he made a journey to the north, passing first from the noble forests with which we are familiar, to those of stunted growth, and finally leaving them behind altogether, at length arriving at the barren and bleak regions beneath the Arctic Circle. In approaching the mountain summits, one is first struck by the appearance of the firs and spruces, which gradually become

MORE AND MORE DWARFISH,

At length rising but a few feet from the ground, the branches spreading out horizontally many feet, and becoming thickly interwoven. These present a comparatively dense upper surface, which is often firm enough to walk upon. At length these disappear wholly, and give place to the Lapland rhododendron, Labrador tea, dwarf birch, and Alpine willows, all of which, after rising a few inches above the ground, spread out over the surface of the nearest rock, thereby gaining warmth, which enables them to exist in spite of tempest and cold. These in their turn give place to the Greenland sandwort, the diapensia, the cassiope, and others, with arctic rushes, sedges, and lichens, which flourish on the very summit.

ARARAT IN AMERICA.

According to Binton's *Myths of the New World*, the tradition of the deluge was held by 28 of the aboriginal tribes of North and South America. The Indians in this section believed that Mt. Washington was the place where a few found a place of safety, and escaped.

TIME'S CHANGES ON MT. WASHINGTON.

In 1642 the first ascension of Mt. Washington was made by Darby Field; in 1810 Abel and Ethan Allen Crawford made the first path to the summit; the bridle-path was made in 1819, and Abel Crawford rode the first horse up, exclaiming, "Can it be possible that a live horse stands on the summit of Mount Washington!" The first house was built by the Crawfords; the old Summit House was put up in 1852 and the Tip-top house in 1853; the carriage-road was finished in 1861, the railroad in 1869, and the present Summit house in 1870.

THE ASCENSION

Of Mt. Washington is *la creme de la creme* of the mountain experience, however. The railway and bridle path run up from the west side, but for beauty and variety of scenery nothing equals the carriage-road from the Glen. Having satisfied yourself by looking through the telescope at the Glen House, that the speck upon the distant summit is the Summit House, where you hope after a four or five hours' ride to take dinner, it will behoove you to put a shawl or overcoat *under* and yourself *upon* the seat of the carriage at the door, and allow the driver to give free rein to his team of six horses. The technical term for *ascending* the mountain is "*attacking*" the mountain. The attack, then, in this instance, is to be from the Glen, and over a fine road that belongs to a stock company.

RIDING UP STAIRS.

From the toll gate to the summit the grade is a constant ascent, varying from 5 to 25 degrees, and for the first third of the distance is buried in the dense foliage of the forests upon the lower side. The sultry temperature of the valley below is exchanged for the exhilarating mountain air, which becomes cool and bracing. It is wholly unlike and distinct from any lowland air, and will be breathed in with delight as a new and enjoyable experience.

As you ascend you will see that the mountain ash, with its scarlet berries, and other small varieties of trees are sub-

HALF-WAY HOUSE, MT. WASHINGTON.

stitutes for the great forest trees near the base.

THE FIRST VIEW

Is a great satisfaction, although you take it by "snatches," the brush upon the side of the road being tall enough to frequently interrupt the view. Finally, at the

HALF-WAY HOUSE,

The prospect becomes suddenly opened, and a vast panorama of indescribable grandeur and beauty invites attention, and—generally receives what it asks for.

The vocabulary of exclamations that are here thrown on the wind, is much too "numerous" for the limits of this guide-book. The accumulation of "Ohs!" and "Ahs!" and the like, that have been prepared by constant practice on the earlier part of the ride, will soon be expended, and the excursionist will sit in silence before the impressive scene, realizing only the quick heart-beats and the inability to express the natural emotions. It is only a step, however

MT. WASHINGTON RAILWAY.

FROM THE SUBLIME TO THE RIDICULOUS,

For, if you do all your predecessors have done, and strict orthodoxy requires, you will get out at the Half Way House (a little wood shanty), and ask the "landlord" (who cooks for the workmen upon the carriage road), if he has any spruce gum?

THEY ALL DO IT,

And you might as well unbend your dignity at this point of the trip, and follow in this time-honored custom and invest in "ten cents worth of gum." From this point, tourists are usually observed to develop facial "gestures" that cannot wholly be ascribed to emotion, and an inclination to expectorate, not wholly attributable to the change in temperature.

SHAWLS AND OVERCOATS

Are generally donned before proceeding, and found to be seasonable and comfortable. Little vegetation is passed on the remainder of the ascent, except "scrubs," whose gnarled roots seem to be crawling over the rocks like so many snakes; short evergreens with their limbs reaching towards the south, which show the direction and power of the winds in winter; and lastly, the mosses and tiny daisies on the very summit.

STEPPING HEAVENWARD.

So greatly do the views enlarge as you progress, that you feel chagrined at having exhausted your very best remarks on so inferior an occasion as you now feel the Half Way House to have been, and you realize that you have now either to repeat (which William S. *never* did) or to let it be inferred by your silence and indifference that you could very easily express yourself if, like Sairey Gamp, you felt so "disposed."

MT. WASHINGTON RAILWAY.

Try to get to the summit by 2 P. M., as at this time the train, which makes two round trips a day, will start down the west side. The times for the train's starting *from the base* is at 10 A. M. and 5:15 P. M., and at 7 A. M. and 2 P. M. *from the summit*. This railway is 6⅔ miles long and rises over 5,000 feet in making the ascent. The fare is three dollars up the mountain, three dollars down, or four dollars up and down on the same train. Since its completion in 1869, over 60,000 passengers have ascended by it and not one of them was injured, a fact that speaks well for its safety.

OTHER INCLINE RAILWAYS.

In Europe there are six cog railroads; the Vitznau-Rigi, the Arth-Rigi, the Rorschach-Heiden and the Ostermandingen, in Switzerland; the Schwabenberg, in Hungaria; and the Khalenberg in Austria. The first two are for the ascension of the famous Mount Rigi. The Vitznau-Rigi,

SUMMIT HOUSE, MT. WASHINGTON.

on the east side, is 4 34-100 miles long, and rises 4,625 feet, costing $130,000 per mile; the Arth-Rigi, on the west side, is 7½ miles long, and rises 4,200 feet. The third the road Rorshach-Heiden, at Lake Bodensee, was opened for traffic in 1875. It cost $450,000, and is 3 32-100 miles long, and rises 1,239 feet. The fourth, the road near Ostermandingen in Switzerland, is ascended by either a friction or cog-wheel engine. It is 1 24-100 miles long. The road up Schwabenberg near Ofen, Hungaria, was built on account of land, as a large amount of real estate on top of Mt. Schwabenberg could be sold thereby. The last of the six, the road up Kehlenberg near Vienna, in Austria, cost nearly $250,-000. Each train runs three cars, and they can carry 15,000 people per day.

THE SUMMIT HOUSE

Is the first place sought after arriving at the summit, and a circle with extended hands gathers around the stoves, for the thermometer will probably stand at about 45°.

GETTING WARM, SUMMIT OF MT. WASHINGTON.

In 1877 the record shows a fluctuation between 40° and 60° with 50° as an average. The snow fell on the 22d of June and 3d of September of that year, but none between. The hotel is a long, low, white frame building, securely chained to the rocks. It contains one hundred sleeping rooms, well furnished, and warmed by steam, so that its patrons are as comfortable and as well served as at any hotel among the mountains. The table is first-class, and Mrs. J. W. Dodge, manager, states that no pains will be spared to make its patrons feel that they can pass a day or a night above the clouds with as much comfort as they can below.

AMONG THE CLOUDS.

There are three buildings of interest to the tourists on the summit of Mt. Washington—the signal service station and the office of the only daily paper ever published among the clouds. It is called *Among the Clouds*, and is edited and printed in the old Tip Top House (that was formerly the only hotel on the summit,) by Henry E Burt If the excursionists will register their names and addresses at the Summit House, they will be printed in the paper, copies of which can be obtained before descending.

DISTANT VIEWS.

The following places may be seen from the summit after a little patient study:

Mt. Beloeil; 135 miles north, 45 degrees west, and nearly over Prospect Hill, Lancaster.

Lake Memphremagog; 70 miles north, 40 degrees west, over Jefferson Hill.

Mount Carmel; 65 miles north, 10 degrees east, and just over Mount Adams.

Mount Bigelow; 70 miles north, 35 degrees east and nearly over Mount Hayes.

Mount Abraham; 65 miles north, 40 degrees east, to the right of Mount Hayes.

Mount Katahdin; 163 miles north, 45 degrees east, and about half way between Mount Hays and Mount Moriah. This is one of the highest of the Adironacks, rising to a height 4,000 feet.

Mount Mansfield; 78 miles north, 78 degrees west, and between the Twin Mountain House and Mount Deception. It is the highest of the Green Mountains, being 4,300 feet high, and appears as a long ridge bearing a fancied resemblance to a human face.

BUILDING THE MONUMENT.

Mount Blue; 57 miles north, 57 degrees east, and half way between Surprise and Moriah.

Portland; 65 miles south, 51 degrees east, and over the northern summit of Doublehead It appears as a low white hill, with a long light blue line beyond it. With a telescope the hill resolves itself into a mass of closely packed white houses, and the blue line is seen to be thickly studded with sails. The ocean, however, is not as often seen as some more distant objects in other directions partly because the atmosphere in this direction seems generally to be somewhat thicker than elsewhere.

Lake Sebago; 43 miles south, 48 degrees east, and over Mount Gemini. It is 14 miles long, and about 11 wide.

Mount Agamenticus; 80 miles south, 24 degrees east.

Isles of Shoals; 97 miles south, 22 degrees east They are very difficult to see, and are situated on the horizon just to the right of Agamenticus.

Kilington peaks; 91 miles south 59 degrees west, and between Mounts Liberty and Blue.

Camel's Hump; 80 miles north, 87 degrees west, and just over Bethlehem. It is a striking looking mountain, shaped like a truncated cone.

Mount Whiteface; 130 miles north, 86 degrees west.

ACCESSIBLE POINTS OF INTEREST.

Among the places that can be reached from the summit, are Tuckerman's Ravine where can be seen the Fall of a Thousand Streams, the Lake of the Clouds, the Great Gulf, Huntington's Ravine, the Alpine Garden, and many others equally interesting. Excursions to these points give a far better idea of the wildness and vastness of this mountain peak than any description can do. *No one should attempt to visit them without a competent guide, however.*

NOT TOO HIGH FOR LITIGATION.

More than $25,000 has been spent in lawsuits about the ownership of the top of the mountain, the contestants being a Mr. Bellows, of Exeter, and Coe & Pingree, of Salem and Bangor. The latter finally compromised by purchasing Bellows' claims.

THE GENERAL VIEW

Has justly been called "an epic landscape." The English Alpestrian, Latrobe, said that it is magnificent, but gloomy. The view-line sweeps around a circumference of nearly 1,000 miles, embracing parts of five States and the Province of Quebec. Within the vast circle are seen scores of villages and hamlets, and hundreds of mountains, with the widening valeys of the chief rivers of New Engand. If the peak was 5,000 feet higher, the beauty of the view would be seriously impaired by the indistinctness caused by the greater distance.

THE CLOUD SCENES.

It would be a misfortune indeed *not* to witness the wonderful transformations of clouds that are often spread out beneath the level of the summit, in the most active and beautiful of panoramas. The writer once witnessed a thunder-storm over the valley south-east of the summit, when the tops of the clouds were lower than the rocks from which it was viewed.

THE EVENING NEWS MONUMENT

Was an enterprise begun in 1878 by last year's excursion party. It is located on a favorable point to the north west of the Tip Top House, and to one insensible to the possibilities of the future may seem not unlike a pile of stones. It *is* a monument, however, for over it Mr. Burt made an oration, and about it the builders gathered to sing, cheer and otherwise dedicate it so that now there is little to distinguish it from Bunker or any other *regularly* dedicated monument, except its name, and the fact that it is the *highest* monument in America.

THE DESCENT

Is made in one quarter of the time it takes to make the ascent. the eight miles from the Summit House to the Glen House being frequently made in less than one hour.

GLEN ELLIS FALLS,

Five miles west of the Glen House, is one of two superb and most picturesque falls in the Ellis river; the other being the Crystal Cascade, which is but three miles from the Glen House. No visit to the mountains is complete without a trip to these exquisite natural gems of scenery. Let the one who considers this exaggerated go and look at them, and—doubt no more. Glen Ellis is 90 and the Crystal Cascade 110 feet high, and no combination of water, rocks, ferns, moss and woods could be more artistic.

GLEN ELLIS FALLS.

LEAVING THE MOUNTAINS.

It will be difficult to express the regret with which the stages for Gorham will be taken. The mountains become friends, and two days seem all too brief to visit with *such* friends. No one is obliged, however, to go on with the excursion, but any and all may remain, and complete the tour leisurely on any regular train. The stages will have to be taken in time to catch the 8:53 A. M. train at Gorham. Saturday, July 12th.

SHELBOURNE

Is five miles from Gorham. To the right of the station is seen the Winthrop House, with Mt. Winthrop towering over it. Granny Starbird's Ledge is passed just before reaching the station.

GILEAD,

Which is the first town we reach in the State of Maine, is six miles from Shelbourne Station. It is hemmed in by lofty mountains. Fine views of Mts Washington, Adams and Jefferson may be had from the right.

WEST BETHEL

Is ten miles nearer Portland. When within five miles of the station, the train passes Tumble Down Dick and crosses Wild River on a bridge 250 feet long Just before arriving at West Bethel the railway crosses Pleasant River Concerning this scenery Starr King wrote: "If the railroad approached no nearer to Gorham than this point, a stage-ride along the same route could hardly be rivaled in New Hampshire. What a delightful avenue to the great range it would be! The brilliant meadows, proud of their arching elms; the full, broad Androscoggin, whose charming islands on a still day rise from it like emeralds from liquid silver: the grand Scotch-looking hills that guard it; the firm lines of the White Mountain ridge that shoot. now and then, across the north, when the road makes a sudden turn; and at last, when we reach Shelbourne, the splendid symmetry that bursts upon us when the mass of Madison is seen throned over the valley itself overtopped by the ragged pinnacle of Adams."

BETHEL.

The railroad leaves the Androscoggin River at this place, a companionship we shall be loath to abandon. Locke Mountain lies to the left and Sparrow Hawk Mountain on the right. In the extreme right are the peaks of Speckled Mountain and the Sunday River White Cap.

LOCKE'S MILLS,

Is the name of a station 65 miles from Portland, located near South Pond. After passing the station the train crosses Alder Stream, along which are some beautiful glens.

BRYANT'S POND,

Which is 700 feet above the] level of the sea, lies near the base of Mt. Christopher. It boasts, also of a water view, i. e., the pond from which it is named.

WEST PARIS.

Is 55 miles or about two hours¼from Portland. To the left the town of

Paris may be seen on the side of the distant hills. Just before reaching the station, the railroad goes down a steep grade of 60 feet to the mile. The next nine stations are of no special importance to the tourist, and will be omitted from this description.

FALMOUTH

Is, within five miles of Portland, near Casco Bay, which may be seen on the left. The salt breezes will be more "visible," however, than the salt water. Just beyond Falmouth, the train crosses the Presumpscott River on a bridge 300 feet long. Passing through the town of Westbrook, the R. R. crosses Back Cove and Munjoy Hill, and arrives at Portland.

THE EASTERN TERMINATION.

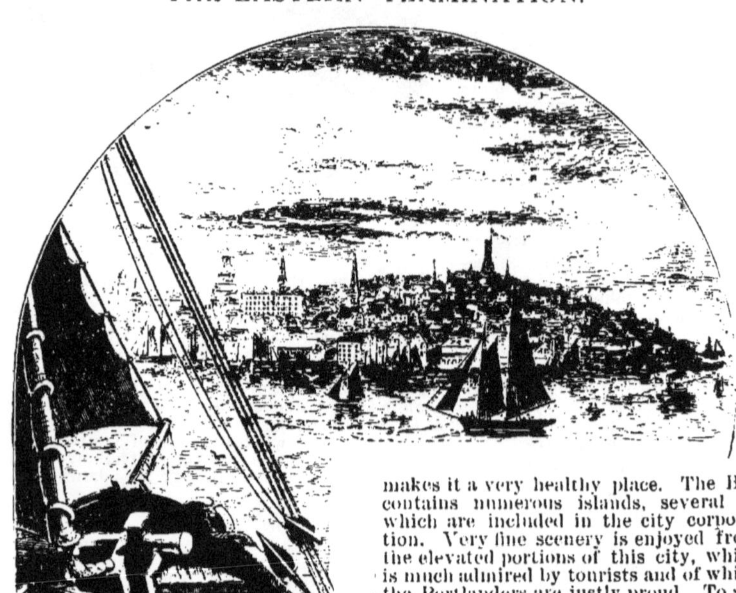

PORTLAND, FROM THE HARBOR.

PORTLAND is gained at 1 P. M. Saturday, July 12th. It is the largest city in Maine. and here we shall get our first glimpse of the sea. It is a pretty, well-built town, with many very elegant residences. It is located on a little peninsula, extending easterly into Casco Bay, and, as the average width of this neck is not more than ¾ of a mile, one does not have to go very far from any part of the city to reach the salt water. The land rises from the sides into a kind of ridge and at its ends are two quite high hills. The tide comes up on both sides of Portland, and the elevation of the city affords excellent facilities for drainage, and makes it a very healthy place. The Bay contains numerous islands, several of which are included in the city corporation. Very fine scenery is enjoyed from the elevated portions of this city, which is much admired by tourists and of which the Portlanders are justly proud. To see the surrounding country and the sea to advantage, the visitor should go to Munjoy's Hill and to the top of the Observatory standing there, and use the telescope placed there for the purpose of watching the ships far out at sea.

THE FIRST SETTLEMENT

Was made here in 1632, by an English colony, but it was not incorporated as a town until 1786. It became a city in 1832. Its population is in the neighborhood of 40,000. Portland boasts of being the birthplace of many celebrities, prominent among whom are Henry W. Longfellow, N. P. Willis, and his sister "Fanny Fern." Longfellow's childhood home can still be seen on Hancock street, corner of Fore,

THERE ARE TWO DEPOTS

In Portland, to which the Grand Trunk Railroad runs. The first is that of the

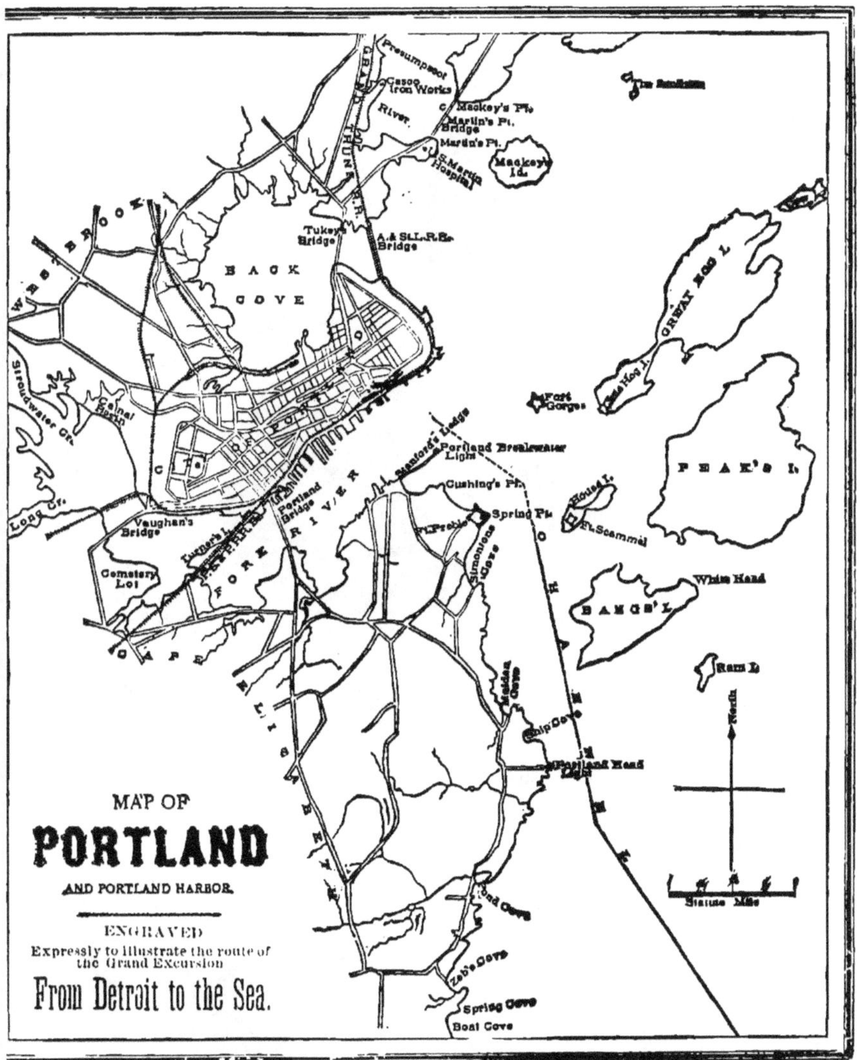

MAP OF
PORTLAND
AND PORTLAND HARBOR.
ENGRAVED
Expressly to illustrate the route of
the Grand Excursion
From Detroit to the Sea.
Presumpscot
Casco Iron Works
River
Mackey's Pt.
Martin's Pt. Bridge
Martin's Pt.
Mackey's Id.
Tukey's Bridge
A.& St.L.R.R. Bridge
BACK COVE
WESTBROOK
GREAT HOG I.
Fort Gorges
Stroudwater Cr.
Canal Basin
Portland Breakwater Light
PEAK'S I.
Cushing's Pt.
House I.
Portland Bridge
Spring Pt.
Ft. Scammel
Vaughan's Bridge
Ft. Preble
Long Cr.
FORE RIVER
Simonton's Cove
Cemetery Lot
White Head
BANGS' I.
CAPE ELIZABETH
Ram I.
North
Maiden Cove
Ship Cove
Portland Head Light
Statute Mile
Pond Cove
Zeb's Cove
Spring Cove
Boat Cove

OBSERVATORY, PORTLAND.

HALF-DAY AT PORTLAND.

May be spent very pleasantly by those who are fond of aquatic diversions by taking a sail boat at the Ferry dock, and going through the shipping, and visiting the breakwater light-house, Forts Gorges, Preble, and Scammel, also will be interesting places to any person not accustomed to the grim habiliments of war. The water is always calm enough to sail out to the head-lights, and Cape Cottage, from which points the ocean view is superb, with its distant sail and countless waves smiling to the sun. Cape Cottage and vicinity can also be reached by carriage drive down Cape Elizabeth.

For 25 cents, a tour of all the islands in the harbor can be made in the little steamer, from Custom House Wharf.

Boston & Maine Railway, where those who intend going direct to the Beach will want to change cars. If baggage is checked simply to Portland, without the depot being specified, it will go on to the next depot. Those changing cars at the first depot will therefore have to see that their baggage is put off by speaking to the baggage master before arriving at Portland. The second depot is about one half block from the dock of the line of steamers that runs each night to Boston; it is also about eight blocks from the Falmouth House, which will be general headquarters during the day.

PORTLAND HEAD-LIGHT.

WHITE-HEAD, PORTLAND HARBOR.

WHITE HEAD—CUSHING'S ISLAND.

On the United States coast survey charts of Portland Harbor, Cushing's Island is styled "Bang's Island," a name by the way, that is essentially inappropriate, as it is a very quiet and picturesque spot. White Head is one of the points of this island that should be visited. It presents to the sea a precipice of from 100 to 150 feet in height, and against it the ocean lashes itself into white foam—hence the name—in its vain effort to break down this natural break-water and safeguard to the harbor. Do not fail as suggested to take the little harbor steamer, that touches at each of these islands, making the round trip in about two hours, for twenty-five cents.

SIDE-TRIP TO BOSTON.

ADVANTAGEOUS rates have been obtained for a side trip from Portland to Boston, via the steamers of the Portland Steam Packet Company and return by the Boston and Maine R. R. The tickets can be obtained at the office of the company which is about a block from the depot. No better use can be made of the four days that are allowed at Portland, (the Eastern terminus of the excursion proper) than to take the nine hours' ride on the Atlantic ocean, which in July is not apt to see much rough weather.

After spending the Sabbath and Monday in Boston, the cars of the Boston and Maine R. R. can be taken, which will give transportation in about four hours to Old Orchard Beach, which is on the sea shore, eleven miles south of Portland. The price of the round trip will be $4.00. The tickets will be good to stop over at Boston and Old Orchard Beach.

BOSTON.

This old and beautiful city, the "Hub" of American literary and musical culture, is too well known to need description. The merest skeleton only of facts and dates will be given, which will readily be filled in from the reader's memory. The first white resident, was the Rev. John Blackstone, who arrived in 1623. In 1635 he sold his claim to the peninsula, where Boston now stands, for £30, and removed

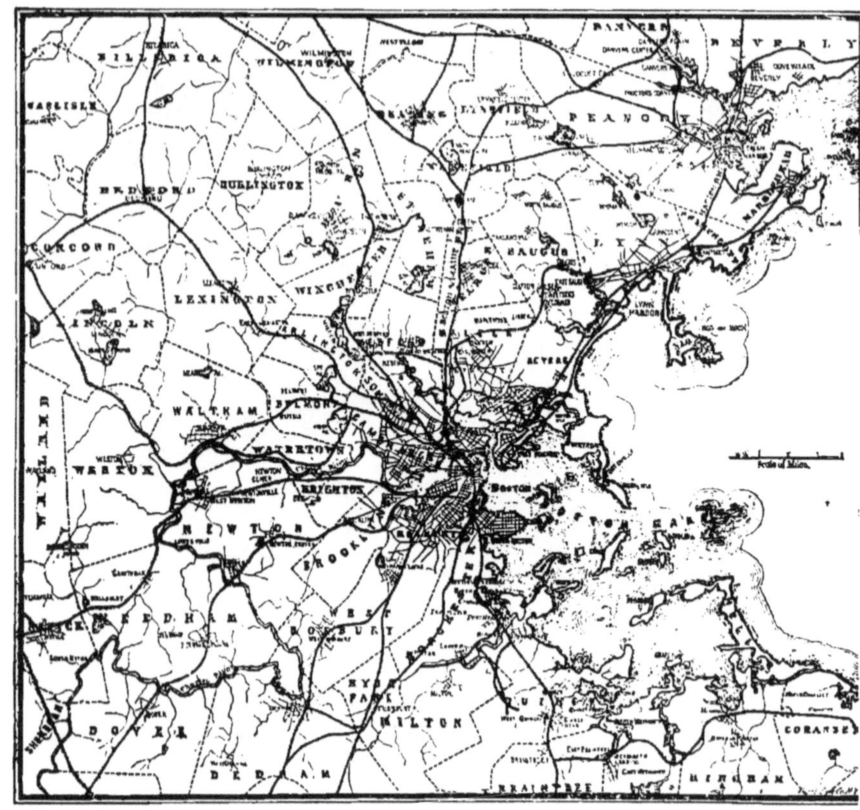

BOSTON AND VICINITY.

to Rhode Island. April 24th, 1704, the first newspaper, the *Boston News Letter*, began publication; March 5th, 1770, was the Boston Massacre, and in 1773 the tea was thrown into the harbor by men disguised as Indians. The city was incorporated in 1822 with a population of 45,000. The population in 1876 was 341,919, but even this gives but a slight idea of the real growth and importance of this famous city, for it is surrounded by a vast network of independent cities, whose population is largely interested in the business of Boston. The trains that follow each other at intervals of only a few minutes on the dozen railways that center at this city, afford the same opportunity to get in and out from business, that horse cars do in smaller places, so the industries of Boston can hardly be estimated, unless two-thirds of the population of a hundred of the smaller adjacent towns be included.

The ground swept of $80,000,000 worth of property, by the terrible fire of November 9th, 1872, has nearly all been rebuilt in the finest possible manner.

The streets in the oldest part of the town are narrow and exceedingly tortuous. Those in the newer part are broad and as "regular" as the heart of any Philadelphian could desire. Commonwealth Avenue, running parallel with Boylston and Beacon streets, is 240 feet wide, and through the centre runs a long park with rows of trees; on either side are wide drive-ways.

THE BRUNSWICK HOUSE

Is sufficiently described by saying that it is the finest house in Boston. It will be the stopping place of those going on THE EVENING NEWS excursion. The accommodations are superb and ample.

OBJECTS OF ANTIQUARIAN INTEREST.

Among "buildings with a history," the most interesting in the United States, next to Independence Hall, in Philadel-

BRUNSWICK HOUSE, BOSTON.

phia, is Faneuil Hall. This famous edifice, the "cradle of liberty," is in Dock Square, which also has an historical fame because of the meetings of the Revolutionary patriots that were held there. The building was erected in 1742, by Peter Faneuil, a Huguenot merchant, and by him presented to the town. The Old State House, in Washington street, at the head of State street, was erected in 1748, and was for half a century the seat of the "Great and General Court of Massachusetts," being the building of which such frequent mention is made in Revolutionary annals. Christ Church (Episcopal), in Salem street, near Copp's Hill is the oldest church in the city, having been erected in 1722.

THE OLD SOUTH CHURCH,

Corner Washington and Milk streets, is an object of much interest It is of brick, and was built in 1729, on the site where the first edifice of the society had stood since 1669. The church was used as a place of meeting by the heroes of '76, and, during the British occupation of the city, was used as a place for cavalry-drill. Kings' Chapel (Unitarian), corner Tremont and School streets, was founded in 1686. Adjoining the church is the first burying-ground established in Boston. In it are buried Isaac Johnson, "the father of Boston," Governor Winthrop, John Cotton, and other distinguished men.

PUBLIC GARDENS, BOSTON.

PUBLIC GARDENS ADJOINING THE COMMON.

Of course every one visiting Boston will want to walk through the famous old Common; and no one should stop until he has crossed the separating avenue, and taken a stroll through the public gardens which are justly the pride of the residents of this city.

Before leaving Boston, every one should take the horse-cars to

CAMBRIDGE,

Which will pass the present home of the poet, Longfellow, (the former headquarters of Washington during the Revolution) also the famous old Elm Tree under which Washington took command of the American army; and Harvard College, the wealthiest and most noted of American colleges.

It is hardly necessary to add that

BUNKER HILL MONUMENT

Should be visited. The monument may be ascended by steps in the interior, and a view of unrivaled beauty gained from the windows at the top. Not far from Bunker Hill (really "Breed's" hill) is the Charlestown Navy Yard, where iron-clad "monitors" and heavy ordnance may be seen. No visit to Boston is complete that does not include a few hours at the Museum of Fine Arts, near the Brunswick, or a trip to Hull on board one of the little harbor steamers.

TWO DAYS AT THE BEACH.

OLD ORCHARD BEACH.

LEAVING Boston by any regular train on the Boston and Maine R. R. Monday afternoon, July 14th, a short ride of about four hours will bridge the distance between Boston and

OLD ORCHARD BEACH.

This beach is one of the finest of southwestern Maine, and probably the most frequented. The beach here is semi-circular, smooth and hard as a floor, making a magnificent promenade, for those who wish to enjoy to the utmost the majestic sea. This beach affords the best facilities for sea-bathing, from its gradual sloope.

THE OLD ORCHARD HOUSE

Is a fine hotel, fronting the sea for a distance of 300 feet, and has all modern conveniences and improvements. It stands on a hill, and back of it, covering the top of the hill, is a fine grove of evergreens, which the proprietor has improved with seats, walks, etc., for a pleasure ground for his guests. This hotel is four and five stories high, and handsomely finished throughout. Its dining-rooms offer all the attractions of excellent sea-side fare, and the sea-fish of every variety, will be found to possess the flavor of absolute freshness; which cannot always be said of those procured in western markets. This house will be the stopping place of the excursion.

A CLAM-BAKE

Is another thing that visitors to the sea side should always participate in. This is an institution those living far inland can never enjoy at home; it will be something to enjoy *en passant*, and something to remember.

The manager of the excursion will arrange a clam-bake for Tuesday afternoon, July 15th.

SURF-BATHING,

Like the motion to adjourn, is always in

SURF-BATHING.

THE OLD ORCHARD HOUSE, AT OLD ORCHARD BEACH.

order, but will be most enjoyed two or three hours before sunset.

"Two are company, but three are none," may qualify the enjoyment of strolling on the beach in the morning when Romeo and Juliet desire to see what mosses, star or jelly fish, the ebbing tide has left stranded on the sand, but "two" are not "company" while bathing in the surf by any manner of means. Fifty are few enough, but one hundred are better.

When the declining sun crowds the beach with promenaders, then it is that the most bashful and diffident of the ladies of the party will emerge from the little bathing houses, in a costume that would create a positive sensation in the hotel parlor, and striding through the ranks of admiring spectators with a reckless abandon, wade boldly out into the surf. Suffer a suggestion. Let from two to ten take hold of hands in the water "middle deep," facing the audience and with backs to the sea The first wave that rolls in simply buoys, but is not large enough to break. The second, mayhap, is larger and lifts the bathers from their feet; but save breath for the traditional "seventh wave": the result of this encounter will generally be too ludicrous to be seriously described.

RETURNING FROM FISHING.

YACHT FISHING.

Yacht riding and fishing will be found to be among the most enjoyable treats at the sea-shore. The *modus operandi* is as follows: Let eight or ten make up a yacht party and engage any one of the dozen or more yacht proprietors who will be found lying on the sand of the beach when disengaged. The bargain should cover use of fishing tackle and transportation from dry land back to dry land, and for the time intervening, at so much an hour.

The second part consists in the beforementioned proprietor rolling up his pants and otherwise preparing to carry the gentlemen on his back and the ladies in his arms to the small boat, which he will afterwards push through the surf to the yacht, which is lying at anchor out in deeper water.

HOISTING SAIL.

The yacht will skim out to sea, to locations the skipper will recognize as favorable for fishing, where anchor will be cast and fishing by drop-line, over the side of the boat, will be found interesting and oftentimes exciting sport.

The return trip simply reverses the order, and is more conducive to hilarity than decorum.

SEEKING A COOLER CLIMATE.

THE 2 P. M. train on the Grand Trunk Railway at Portland, will be taken Wednesday afternoon, July 16th, and the general direction of the following eighteen hours' travel will be northward, to the latitude of Lake Superior. Supper will be taken at the Alpine House at Gorham

POINT LEVI.

After the fatigue of the day has been slept away in your comfortable bed in the Pullman sleeping car, you think morning has come too soon, as at 6 A. M. the porter wakes you up with the information that you are nearing Point Levi, where you are to leave the cars in order to pass the day in exploring the old city opposite, which will more than meet the expectations of the stranger. Point Levi, which stands on the south bank of the St. Lawrence, opposite Quebec, is the capital of Levis county, and has a population of 7,000. It is the terminus of the Grand Trunk Railway.

A DAY AT QUEBEC.

QUEBEC, FROM POINT LEVI.

LANDING from the ferry, a calash (a unique two wheeled vehicle found only in Quebec) or carriage should be taken for the St. Louis Hotel, which will be excursion headquarters for the day—after breakfast, a carriage that will accommodate five persons can be obtained for $5.00 for the entire day, and as all Quebec hackmen are lecturers as well as drivers, no further suggestions to the tourist are necessary. The steamer for Montreal will leave about 5 P. M., and should be taken in time to secure berths. These may be obtained also at the ticket office opposite the St Johns hotel.

QUEBEC.

So many adjectives have been exhausted upon the beauties and attractions of this old town by tourists, that one scarcely knows how to attempt a description without seeming to plagiarize; but whatever may have been said, the quaintness of the city invariably impresses the tourist who visits it for the first time with a sense of foreignness that makes it difficult for him to believe that he has not left the American continent, contrasting it, as one cannot help doing, with the cities of the United States. Their air of self-satisfied, prosperous modernness makes Quebec appear deliciously crooked, quaint, odd, irregular and fascinating. It is built upon a high bluff and plain that form part of the north bank of the St. Lawrence, or as they call it here,

THE SAN LAURENT,

and upon a low strip of river front to the east of the bluff. The roofs of the houses and buildings are almost invariably of tin, which in the bright sun and clear air of this northern climate flash and sparkle like silver. This brilliant spectacle is best enjoyed from the distance as you drive through the village of Beauport on your way to the Falls of Montmorenci. Here the effect is really dazzling, and you involuntarily think of the descriptions of that City whose streets are of "pure gold, like unto clear glass, and whose walls are garnished with all manner of precious stones." Quebec is divided by its location into the upper and lower towns, the upper including the citadel, being

ENCLOSED BY A WALL

Nearly three miles in length. This was formerly pierced by five gates, now nearly all dismantled.

HISTORICALLY CONSIDERED

It is one of the oldest cities on the continent, having been founded in 1608 by Champlain. Its site was visited in 1535, and possession taken of the land in the name of the French, by Jacques Cartier, who erected there a wooden cross with these words inscribed thereon: Franciscus primus, Dei gratia, Francorum Rex, regnat. Quebec remained the seat of French power in America until the defeat of Montcalm in 1759, and as it has since been the Queen of the St. Lawrence, seated in majesty upon its natural throne of rock, the great fortress of English strength in British America, it must possess great interest for the well-informed tourist.

THE CITADEL,

One of the most impregnable of fortresses, is always of interest to visitors. It crowns the head of the Promontory of Cape Diamond, which is an immense rock 333 feet above the river, whose sides are almost smooth enough to have been hewn, and with its bristling cannon pointing in every direction, completely commands every approach to the city, and gives it the name, "Gibraltar of America" The fortifications are very extensive, covering more than 40 acres; and three quarters of a mile up the river, on the Plains of Abraham, are two Martello Towers, connected with the fort by underground passages. The Citadel is kept in order by British soldiers, who very politely show visitors around, and point out all that is of interest.

DURHAM TERRACE,

In the Upper Town, is a large platform occupying the site of the old castle of St. Louis, which was burned in 1834, and as it commands the same fine prospect it is a favorite promenade. It was erected by Lord Durham, hence its name. In the Public Garden, near by, is the elegant monument which was placed there in 1827, to the memory of both Wolfe and Montcalm, though these two brave enemies fell on the Plains of Abraham, at the close of the memorable battle of Sept. 13, 1759, when Canada was lost to the French and gained for the English. Wolfe died just as the victory was decided, and Montcalm on being told that his wounds were fatal, said: "So much the better, I shall not live to see the surrender of Quebec." The spot where Gen. Wolfe fell is marked by a plain monument on the battle field, and is always visited by tourists. A large part of the Upper City is occupied by the buildings and grounds of great religious corporations, Laval University, the Ursulines and the Hotel-Dieu.

THE ROMAN CATHOLIC CATHEDRAL

Is a large though not very pretentious building, capable of seating 4,000 peasons. The interior is quite handsome, but its chief attractions are its age (it was built in 1647), and the fine paintings by the old masters which it contains. In order to enjoy these the visitor should ask the sexton for a catalogue, which gives the name and location of each picture. He will also, if asked, (not otherwise) show

ARMSTRONG GUN, QUEBEC CITADEL.

the wonderful robes for the priests, made of gold and silver brocade, and jeweled with diamonds and rubies. The Seminary Chapel, connected with this church, contains many fine paintings, and should be visited without fail. There are many other buildings, churches, etc., which it would be interesting to visit if one had the time, but by this time you have pretty well "done" the Upper Town and are ready for dinner. If you take this at the St. Louis Hotel you will see almost opposite you, a little to the west, the old one-story low-roofed house with dormer windows, where the dead body of poor

A QUEBEC CALASH.

General Montgomery was laid, on that snowy 31st of December, while his young wife, the daughter of Judge Robert Livingston, was waiting for him at their home in the State of New York, where she never more heard his voice.

THE ST. LOUIS HOTEL

Will be the stopping place for the excursion. Mr. Willis Russell, the proprietor, also owns the Russell House.

BEAUPORT.

After your early dinner, or lunch, if you wish to dine later you are ready for a drive to the Falls of Montmorenci, through that quaintest of villages, Beauport. For this, if there are only two of you who wish to go together, take a calash, (which is an institution peculiar to Quebec, being a sort of two-wheeled carriage with a cover, drawn by one horse; which the driver manages very skillfully, going at a great rate through the narrow, crooked streets without once getting caught among the numerous other vehicles, as you would think he must. You pass through a part of the Lower Town, which is the newer portion of Quebec, to the suburb called St. Roche. When you ride through this prosperous manufacturing and mercantile part of the place, remember that 340 years ago it was the

INDIAN VILLAGE OF STADACONA.

And here in 1535 its chief, Donnacona, was taken from his people and carried by Jacques Cartier across the ocean as a gift to Francis I., King of France. Soon after leaving Roche's Ward, as it is called, you turn into the macadamized road to Beauport, first crossing Dorchester Bridge over the St. Charles. Beauport is a single street running parallel with the St. Lawrence for five miles, and far above it. It is a village of long, narrow farms, those on the south side of the street running to the river, while those on the opposite side stretch away to the north. The houses are one story high, nearly all white, and stand with *one corner* to the street, so as to break the force of the fierce winds that sweep up the river in the winter. It is the simplest of villages. There are no stores, no manufactories—nothing but the little homes, surrounded by their neat gardens filled with brave, old-fashioned flowers and vigorous vegetables.

ISLAND OF ORLEANS.

On the road through Beauport a fine view can be had of the island of Orleans, which is 19 miles long. It is a beautiful island, with its dark green woods, fine farms and little white villages.

FALLS OF MONTMORENCI.

After passing through the village of Beauport, your carriage leaves the main road and you pass partly around the estate which, in 1791, was the home of the Duke of Kent, Queen Victoria's father. You can visit his room if you wish to. Crossing a bridge over the Montmorenci river, your carriage stops in

FALLS OF MONTMORENCI.

front of a little hotel, or waiting house, where you leave it, and passing through an enclosure, going a few rods on foot, you soon arrive at the brink of a narrow, deep gorge, which is a gap, or inlet in the northern bank of the St. Lawrence, shaped like the thumb of a mitten, with almost vertical walls of rock entirely around it except where it opens into the St Lawrence. When you stop you are about midway between the opening and the end of this thumb, and directly opposite you, is one of the loveliest of cataracts. In the summer, when the water in the Montmorenci river is comparatively low, the Falls number some 12 or 15 narrow silver ribbons fringed with lace-like spray which against the dark brown rock and abundant green foliage above it, look indescribably beautiful. They are all united in one, when the water is high, and plunge 250 feet to join themselves with the clear green waters of the St. Lawrence. At your feet descends a staircase with frequent landing places, for it is very steep, down which you can go to the very foot of the Falls; for though you are on the opposite side, the gorge is so narrow, that the spray will dash over you as you look up. After satisfying yourself with the beauty and grandness of the scene, for it combines the two qualities, you will find the drive back to the city pleasant and will have just about time to go to your hotel and gather up your effects in time for the boat to Montreal, which leaves the wharf at precisely 5 o'clock P. M.

PLAN YOUR DAY.

By asking the porter at the Hotel to get you a carriage as soon as you have had your breakfast in the morning, and going in clubs, two for a calash, and five or six for a hack, excursionists can easily visit all the places above described, taking them in the order mentioned, and probably might visit some of the many other places of interest in or near Quebec, if they planned to do so, and tried to be expeditious, and still be ready for the 5 o'clock boat.

OFF FOR MONTREAL.

Not the least delightful part of the day is its closing hours on the St. Lawrence. The two boats that run between Montreal and Quebec are named after these cities, and are about on a par with the Hudson River steamers; in other words, are immense floating palaces. The views along the banks of the river are so fine that one feels as if he must not lose the time during the three hours of daylight to go below for supper, but when he does go he finds the supper good and well served.

SIDE TRIP TO THE SAGUENAY.

A SIDE trip has been arranged with tickets at $10.00 for a three days' trip by steamer from Quebec down the St. Lawrence to the mouth of the Saguenay, thence up the Saguenay to and 40 miles beyond Ha Ha Bay. Thus, instead of returning to Montreal by steamer on the afternoon of the 17th of July, (Thursday) the Saguenay steamer can be substituted, which returns to Quebec on Monday, July 21st. The price of ticket ($10) is a special one to members of the excursion only, and includes state-room and meals.

OFF FOR THE SAGUENAY

The St. Lawrence only begins to show itself in its full majesty below Quebec. After passing the Island of Orleans in one of the luxurious steamers of the St. Lawrence steam navigation company one finds the narrow channel broadening out into a mighty stream whose opposite shores can barely be discerned from the promenade deck. But let him take a parting glance at Quebec from the basin, and note what a splendid picture she makes; Cape Diamond towering up to her crown of battlements, the city with spire and dome rising above the shining roofs, then to the south the uplands of Levis sloping away in terraces to the borders of Maine. To the north the Valley of the St. Charles, the long white line of Beauport, with the Falls, first seen as a slender white thread tumbling down, then as a broad band, then as a curtain, vanishing as the head of the Island of Orleans is swept into view. This island is 20 miles long and about five miles wide. It has been under cultivation in parts for over two centuries, and has a population of about 7,000.

Below the island, on the mainland, the Laurentian Mountains form the north shore of the river. Cap Tourmente is the first spur of any magnitude seen It is a bold, picturesque bluff, 1,900 feet high. The quarantine station of Grosse Isle is a charming island, claiming attention from the fact that it was one of the barriers to the cholera in the epidemic years. When ship fever swept off the Irish immigrants fleeing from the famine, Grosse Isle became a terrible lazar house. In one grave on that island lie 7 000 victims to the fever

Numerous beautiful islands swarming with wild fowl are passed. The historical Baie St. Paul, guarded by Isle Aux Coudres, or Hazel' Island, swings into sight, and at the landing uncouth specimens of rural French Canadians will afford the tourist opportunity for study. From here to Murray Bay, a famous watering place, the scenery is of the most enchanting character; the eye feasts upon beauty with every mile of progress made. Ten miles below the bay The Pilgrims, a curious group of islands, will be pointed out. They are visible at a great distance, and what is remarkable, seldom present the same appearance twice to the beholder. The mirage is constantly present in the neighborhood of these rocks.

Riviere du Loup, or Fraserville, is the terminus of the Intercolonial Railway, whence communication may be had by rail with Halifax and St. John, N. B. Two splendid waterfalls can be seen at Riviere du Loup, which is a charming summer resort. After a stoppage at Cacouna, the Newport of Canada, the most fashionable of summer resorts, a run of 20 miles due north brings us to Tadousac, at the mouth of the Saguenay. This will be about evening, and the tourist will find the advantage of some warm wraps. If the day has been warm the breeze from the Saguenay will come down laden with heat, however, from the radiation of the warmth absorbed by the rocks.

The Saguenay is a tremendous cleft in the Laurentian range, apparently the consequence of some awful convulsion of nature. Tadousac, at its mouth, is an older settlement than Quebec, and has a church which is the most ancient on the continent. The place is very fashionable, and the sea bathing superb. The St. Lawrence here is as salt as the sea. The scenery is simply gorgeous. Mountain, forest and flood going to make up a whole which cannot well be described in restricted space. From this point to Chicoutimi, about 100 miles, the highest point to which the steamer ascends, there is hardly a foot of the way lacking in interest and grandeur. Almost at every turn new beauties are discovered; here a placid bay, there a green island rising out of the dark waters, yonder foaming cascades, tumbling over precipitous rocks, a quarter of a mile at a bound! The shores rise from the water in inaccessible cliffs, brown and bare save for here and there a scrambling dwarf pine or a few blue-berry bushes. There is no beach. In some places the steamer might run beside the rocks and have 1,000 feet of water under her keel. It is remarkable that the Saguenay is very much deeper than the St. Lawrence. Into some of its depths plummet has never yet found bottom.

All is rugged, huge and impressive in this mysterious river. Two appalling headlands are those which guard the entrance to Eternity Bay, Capes Trinity and Eternity. Cape Trinity is composed of three immense bluffs, some 1900 feet high. Cape Eternity is but little inferior in height, and neither have equals in rugged majesty in the world. One feels, when the steamer glides by, a sort of sensation that the rock is about to topple over. The echoes in the Saguenay are superb and astonishing. As Ha Ha is reached and the vessel steams across its land-locked waters, one begins to feel a regret at not being able to stay and have a shy at the numerous accessible amusements of shooting, fishing, swimming. But the stoppage is short, and after a few hours' stay we move on to Chicoutimi, at the foot of Lake St. John. The return voyage is equally pleasing with the descent, for the boats are excellently kept, the table is luxurious, the hotels along the route well kept, and the company generally entertaining.

SIDE-TRIP TO SARATOGA.

WHILE at Montreal, after the return from Quebec by steamer on the St. Lawrence, (one of the most enjoyable portions of the route, as the steamers are little short of floating palaces) two or three days could not be more profitably spent than in taking a run "up" to Saratoga and back. Side trip tickets will be for sale to those holding our general excursion tickets only, at the ticket stand in the office rotunda of the Windsor Hotel. The tickets will be good either way by steamer or railway, and for the round trip from Montreal to Saratoga and return the price will be $12.50.

The tourist can hardly select a route anywhere in this country upon which in the same distance there is so much to be seen of deep interest as that from Montreal, through Lake Champlain and Lake George, to Saratoga and return. Some of the finest lake scenery in the world is enjoyed, while the route lies through the most stubbornly contested regions of the revolutionary war, and is rich in antiquarian remains. Besides all this the tourist has a glimpse of the most fashionable watering-place life on the American continent.

Leaving Montreal, the first object to attract attention is the magnificent Victoria bridge upon which we cross to the south bank of the St. Lawrence. Some very pretty country engages our attention till we reach

THE NATIONAL BOUNDARY,

Two hours ride from Montreal. The line here is not marked by any natural conformation of river or mountain range,

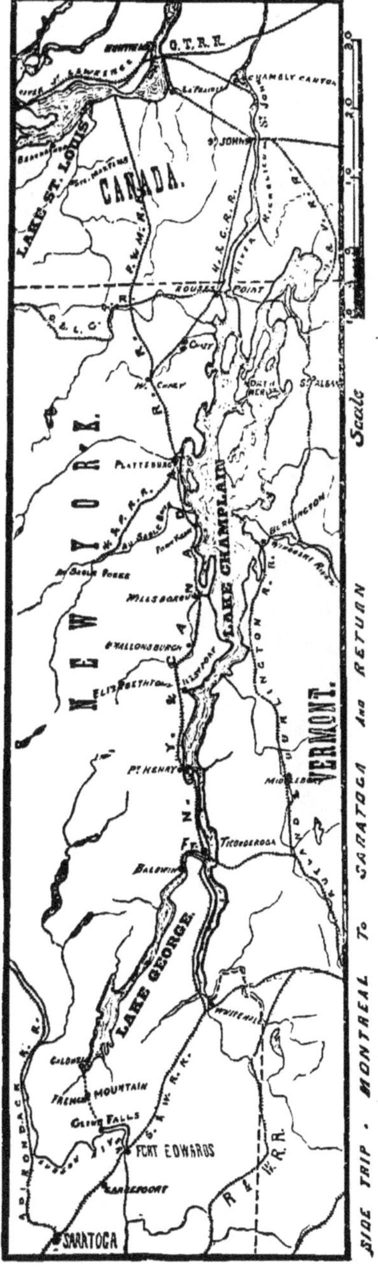

but is simply an arbitrary line like that dividing one township from another. It will be pointed out, however, by the brakeman or conductor, and is an object of interest to most travelers. At the point where this line crosses the River Richelieu the outlet of Lake Champlain, stands the old revolutionary fort Montgomery, still maintained by the United States government as commanding the outlet of Lake Champlain, and which may easily be seen from the railroad.

At Plattsburg we may, if we choose, take a branch road to

THE FAMOUS AU SABLE CHASM.

One of the grandest canons to be found east of the Rocky Mountains; or if we desire to push on we have the option of continuing our journey by rail or taking the steamer on Lake Champlain. If we take the rail we shall have more time at Fort Ticonderoga, and those of antiquarian tastes will select that mode of travel; but all who want to enjoy the most magnificent half day's steamboating they ever experienced will remain over night at Plattsburg, and bright and early next morning take the fine steamer Vermont for

A SAIL UP LAKE CHAMPLAIN.

The lake is narrow and smooth. On either side rise grandly the Green Mountains of Vermont and the Adirondacks of New York. We touch at Burlington, the chief city of the Green Mountain State, but all our other stops are on the west or New York shore of the lake. At Fort Henry extensive iron works attract the attention, and a little beyond, the old fortifications of Crown Point, which the reader of revolutionary history will associate with the early scenes of the war. They should be pointed out by the captain, as they are not identical with the stopping place known as Crown Point. A fine dinner is obtainable on the boat, and soon thereafter the lake narrows to a mere river, and, metaphorically, we pass under the guns of

FORT TICONDEROGA.

Its ruined buildings are plainly seen from the boat, but the distance is such from the landing place that they are not easily visited unless we stop over on purpose. Fort Ticonderoga was probably the strongest fortification that figured in revolutionary history, unless it be that of Quebec. It was built by the French just prior to their surrender of Canada to the British, and is said to have cost some millions of dollars.

A short bit of railroad carries us up an elevation of 240 feet to Baldwin, at the foot of

LAKE GEORGE,

The most beautiful and romantic lake in America. Its banks are lined with moun-

AU SABLE CHASM.

fortable chair on the 333-feet-long piazza. A before-breakfast climb to the top of the neighboring Prospect Mountain, 2,000 feet high, will give one an undoubted appetite. Another little antiquarian exploration is had among the ruins of Fort George, a relic of the French war and of Sir William Johnson's admirable Indian administration.

From Fort William Henry old-time 4-horse stages carry us over a pleasant country road to

GLENS FALLS

On the Hudson, one of the most important water-powers and lumber manufacturing places in New York State. A lay-over here for one train will well repay the traveler. Here we take the train again, follow the river, with its jams of logs, reminding one of our Michigan rivers at certain seasons, for some distance in a southerly direction, then strike across the country to

SARATOGA,

The Baden Baden of America. No matter how much a stranger to fashionable life one may be he can hardly fail to enjoy a stay of a day or two at this place. The mineral waters are most refreshing, particularly those of the Congress Spring, and are free

tains often rising precipitously hundreds of feet. The lake is narrow and winding, affording a constantly changing view, and its shores and numerous islands are dotted over with scores of pretty little cottages the summer homes of wealthy New Yorkers. Lake George is identical with Horicon Lake of Cooper's novels. The lake is 36 miles long and the ride up it the event of a life time. At the head is the village of Caldwell and

FORT WILLIAM HENRY HOTEL,

An immense summer caravansary capable of accommodating 400 guests and admirably kept. In the parlors and on the spacious piazzas of an evening we get a capital glimpse of the luxury of fashionable life—music, dancing, promenading, boating on the lake, and quiet enjoyment of the surroundings in a com-

to all. The streets and hotels are thronged with beauty and gaiety, and so much of life and brilliancy is seldom seen so closely congregated elsewhere. The whole town overflows with it, and the transient guest, though a stranger, cannot fail to enjoy the experience, The hotels of Saratoga rank quite among the wonders of the world. The three leading ones—the Grand Union, the United States and Congress Hall--have a capacity for 2,500 guests each, and these are only three out of about fifty.

THE RETURN TO MONTREAL

May be varied by stopping off either at Westport or Plattsburg, and staging due west from ten to twenty miles and visiting the well-known and much-frequented resorts in the Adirondack mountains. The mountains lie all along the western shore of lakes Champlain and George, but to get into the very heart of this beautiful and romantic region, the suggestions above will have to be followed. All the previously mentioned portion of this excursion may be taken in with comparative haste, but the inclination of the tourist will now demand the quiet and rest necessary to reflect upon and digest what has been seen. Such a place may be easily found in the nooks of the Adirondacks, for hotels and boarding houses abound on every side

THE VACATION TERMINATES.

THE plans of the sleepers on the G. T. R. R. will be found at the ticket stand in the office rotunda of the Windsor Hotel, Montreal.

Sleepers secured, they should be occupied before 10 P. M., as that is the time for starting west.

ALEXANDRIA BAY, N. Y.,

Which will be passed on the return from Montreal, is merely a widening of the St. Lawrence River, but is filled with a portion of the rocky islands of the Thousand Islands which here find their maximum of beauty. Among the islands of this bay. the most famous fishing and boating "grounds" of the river are situated, and no more delightful way of employing the unexpired portion of the excursion ticket could be found, than to stop off at one of the points on the G. T. R. R. opposite, and take the ferry across the St. Lawrence to the

THOUSAND ISLAND HOUSE,

Which is situated at the head of, and overlooking the bay. This house is strictly first-class in all of its appointments, and has deservedly become a popular Summer resort.

TORONTO.

A day may be profitably spent at Toronto, which will be reached the morning after leaving Montreal. The Queen's Hotel will offer the hospitalities of that interesting city, and afford an excellent resting place.

THE CROSSING AT PORT HURON.

Is at the upper part of St. Clair River, and in sight of Lake Huron. The river at this crossing is very deep and the current quite rapid. A stop of one hour will be made at this place for supper and the examination of baggage by the Custom House officers.

The ladies who have purchased silks, laces, kid gloves etc, etc., in Quebec and Montreal, will have to unlock their trunks with a steady hand and innocent-looking face, else the said officials will become suspicious, and the latter experience of the excursionist will be worse than the first; for not only are smuggled goods confiscated, but the smuggler is generally heavily fined. It remains a lamentable fact, however, that the majority of ladies who do smuggle escape detection.

CALL AT OUR OFFICE.

The proprietors of THE EVENING NEWS will be pleased to see the returning excursionists at the publishing house, No. 65 Shelby street. Detroit, where not the least of the points of interest in the excursion tour will be the press-room of this paper, where, any afternoon between 2 and 5.30 o'clock the printing of the regular edition of 22,000 papers may be witnessed.

EXPRESS YOUR OPINION.

As it is the intention of the manager of this excursion to repeat the tour in 1880, it will be of value as well as a personal satisfaction, to receive a candid and discriminating criticism of the route, management, etc., etc., after their return home, from those who have participated in the "third" annual excursion tour.

SUNDAY-SCHOOL TEACHERS'

FIVE YEARS' RECORD BOOK.

THE demand for increased facilities in Sunday-School work justifies the announcement of the above named work, which has been designed and copyrighted by W. H. BREARLEY, Detroit, Mich.

It contains at least FOUR features that are new and distinct from other forms of record.

First.—The first four pages are devoted to an "enrollment" of the members of the class in the handwriting of the pupils; these signatures follow and subscribe to an agreement concerning attendance, etc.

Second.—From 54 to 104 pages (according to the size of the book) are given for an INDIVIDUAL record, of not only the attendance and absence of the pupil, but of the cause of absence and items of personal history concerning residence, conversion, etc., etc., etc. The manner of keeping this record, which is fully explained in the book, REQUIRES that the teacher become intimately acquainted with each of the pupils, by visiting the absentees.

Third.—Eight pages in the back of the book are given for a record of the history of the class as a whole; such a record would be invaluable to many teachers, who have trusted to, but have been betrayed by, their memory.

Fourth.—The record is PERMANENT, as few pupils remain in one class more than five years, and there are enough pages for new pupils. The book contains an index, and a place for the record of visitors, contributions, and class attendance. As two leaves can be used for the record of a single pupil, the book can be used for a TEN years' record without change.

The book is something entirely new and unique.

It is bound in black cloth, with title embossed in gold letter.

It is as convenient as it is handsome.

The book is the outgrowth of experience rather than a mere theory.

WHAT OTHERS THINK OF IT.

SIMPLE AND COMPREHENSIVE.

"A very compact, comprehensive and simple system for keeping a class register; and very neatly prepared."—[A. T. Pierson, D. D., Detroit, Mich.

AS NEARLY PERFECT AS CAN BE.

"I think your 'Five Years' Class Book' is as nearly perfect as anything can be for the designed purpose. Your book cannot fail to come into demand."
[Rev. N. C. Mallory, Lynn, Mass.

MOST SATISFACTORY.

"I am very glad I came across your Record Book. I have long wished some form of permanent record more satisfactory than any I could find or devise for myself, and yours is the most satisfactory I have ever seen."[—W. R. Hurd, Forestville, Conn.

FOR PRIVATE CONVENIENCE.

"'Sunday-School Teachers' Five Years' Record Book.' Detroit: W. H. Brearley.—This book is of 12mo size. It consists of eleven pages, lettered at the side, for an index; fifty-seven pages for records of individual members, as present or absent; a page each, for records of visitors, class contributions and class attendance; and eight blank pages for general items of class history. It is designed for the private convenience of teachers desiring to preserve a permanent record at home. (12mo, cloth limp. Price, $1.00.)"
[—Philadelphia S. S. Times, Nov. 23, 1878.

LOOKS TO PERMANENCY.

"I have examined your 'Sunday-School Teachers Record Book,' and like it well. Its use will promote order and thoroughness, and, what is of great importance, it looks to permanency in the relation between teacher and pupil."[—Rev. Z. Grenell, Jr., Bay City.

COMPLETE AND PRACTICAL.

"After a personal and careful examination of 'The Sunday-School Teachers' Five Years' Record Book,' by W. H. Brearley, the undersigned takes pleasure in commending it for its comprehensiveness; its systematic and convenient arrangement; and without reservation regards it as the most complete, practical and best 'Sunday-School Teachers' Record Book' with which he is acquainted."
[—Rev. L. H. Trowbridge, "Michigan Christian Herald."

EVERY TEACHER OUGHT TO KEEP IT.

"For the private convenience of those Sunday-school teachers who wish to keep a permanent record of each of their pupils, W. H. Brearley, of the Detroit 'Evening News,' has produced a 'Five Years' Record Book,' which will enable them to do it for the time mentioned in the title. The five years' record is made upon a single page, so that the chronicles for that period can be seen at a glance. Such a record every teacher ought to keep. Detroit: W. H. Brearley, 65 Shelby St. $1.00.—[National Teacher.

PRICE LIST.

Small Size, 60 pages, - - - -	**$1.00**
Medium Size, 84 pages, - - - -	**1.25**
Large Size, 108 pages, - - - -	**1.50**

☞ Copies of this RECORD BOOK will be sent to any address on receipt of price.

W. H. BREARLEY,
65 Shelby St., Detroit, Mich.

ISLAND POND HOUSE, ISLAND POND, VT.,

D. STONE, MANAGER.

—ALSO—

STEWART HOUSE,

ISLAND POND, VERMONT,

D. STONE, MANAGER.

Adjoining the Island Pond House, and connected with it by a covered walk, will be opened for guests.

☞ Trains from Montreal, Quebec and Portland, all stop about one hour for meals. Meals served at all hours. Board from $1.00 to $2.00 per day. Special arrangements made for Board by the week.

☞ Daily Stage from Island Pond to Newport. A good livery connected with the house.

ISLAND POND, VT.

WHAT, AND WHERE IS ISLAND POND?

It is a small village of 1200 inhabitants, in the north-east section of Vermont, close to the Boundary line. It is located on the Grand Trunk Railroad, midway between Montreal and Portland, the distance to each city being 150 miles. A point whereat all trains stop from one to two hours for meals, and the examination of passengers' baggage going in and coming out of Canada. Connected with all parts of the Dominion and the United States by telegraph.

The village is situated on a height of land over 1300 feet above the level of the sea, the dividing point or water shed into the Atlantic to the south and the Gulf of St. Lawrence to the north, and with its noticeably pure and bracing atmosphere, the place is one of the most healthful mountain towns in New England. The country lying about is almost an unbroken wilderness, with clearings however, made by the fire or axe, with a plentiful proportion of mountains and hills.

Mount Bluff, an eminence 1200 feet high, rises abruptly on the north of the village, and from its summit, three miles distant, a magnificent view may be obtained. The White Mountains of New Hampshire, certain parts of the Green Mountain Range, and Owl's Head, rising from the side of Lake Memphremagog, in Canada, are all distinctly visible, with an intervening expanse of forest, mountain, river and lake, which, once seen, can hardly fade from the memory.

The name, Island Pond, implies that there is water near by. The village is located upon the banks of a mountain lake, three and one-half miles long, and one mile wide, and the view of this picturesque sheet of water, with its prominent island in the foreground, is one of the characteristic of the place. During the summer months a small steam yacht plies for the convenience of pleasure parties, while small craft, from the tidy sail boat to the bark canoe, are also to be found, if desired. There are four churches in the place.

To the lover of the rod and line, Island Pond furnishes strong attractions. In the vicinity of the hotels, ranging from one to sixteen miles distant, are fifteen mountain lakes, and numerous streams, which can be reached some by train in twenty minutes, and others by an hour's drive over good roads and through the most picturesque parts of the state. All these waters abound in trout from the small pan fish to the noble three and four pounder, and so easy of access that ladies with a taste for the gentle art, can enjoy a day's trout fishing. To the lover of camp life, tramps of five and ten miles through the forest, with really good fishing at the end, repay him for his exertions.

It remains to say a word as to the boarding accommodations of the place. There are two large hotels, connected by a covered walk, and now under the same management. The older of these, the ISLAND POND HOUSE, has been long and most favorably known to the traveling public. The house with which this is connected, the STEWART HOUSE, is modern in its appointments, and but just finished and opened. This second house alone contains sixty-three sleeping apartments; it has wide and beautiful piazzas from which unsurpassed views of the surrounding country can be obtained.

Its first-class hotel accommodations, beautiful drives and rides, fine boating and fishing, and picturesque scenery, the advantages of two daily mails, telegraph offices, and a direct rail route, cannot fail to render Island Pond the popular resort for the tourist, artist, business man and disciple of Walton.

THE NIAGARA HOUSE,

NIAGARA FALLS.

That portion of the traveling public which has been more or less acquainted with the appearance and hotel accommodations of the Niagara House, at Niagara Falls, during the many years of its existence—a period covering the better portion of Niagara's popularity as an American summer resort—will find that ancient hostelrie so changed in its internal arrangements and furnishing, under its new management, that its former proprietors would hardly recognize the place. Since the retirement of Messrs. Lewis & Davie, and the subsequent decision of Mr. R. D. Porter, the owner of the property, to furnish and run the hotel himself, the house has been thoroughly and completely renovated from cellar to garret. The ceilings have been frescoed, the walls papered, the wood-work painted, the halls and stairways dressed with new carpets, and every room in the house newly fitted up with handsome carpeting, elegant furniture, and every modern hotel convenience. The entrance to the hotel has been enlarged, new doors hung, the windows to the reception-room lowered, the office greatly improved in appearance, the parlors tastefully and handsomely furnished, the bar rearranged and newly fitted up, a barber-shop and wash-room provided, the kitchen thoroughly overhauled, and even the grounds surrounding the hotel have shared in the general renovation of the property. The hotel as it now stands is as neat and cosy a public inn as any visitor with ordinary wants could desire. It is to be run as a $2 per day house, and with the accommodations it furnishes the hotel ought to become very popular with a good portion of the traveling public. The management of the house has been entrusted to Mr. Sanford Wheaton, a gentleman qualified by experience and ability to most satisfactorily discharge the duties of a landlord. Mr. Stewart Porter, a son of the owner of the hotel, is associated with Mr. Wheaton in the management of the house.

DETROIT, GRAND HAVEN & MILWAUKEE

RAILWAY.

(Formerly the Detroit & Milwaukee R. R.)

THE SHORTEST, QUICKEST and MOST DIRECT LINE

From Northern Michigan and the Great Northwest, to

New York, Boston, Buffalo, Albany, Syracuse, Rochester, Philadelphia, Baltimore, Washington, and all points in the Eastern States and Canada.

From Milwaukee and Northwest points to Detroit or any point East, this route will save 100 miles in distance, $3.00 in Railway fare and $2.00 for sleeping-car fare.

Passengers to and from Chicago will find this a pleasant Summer Route which will enable them to enjoy a pleasant sail on Lake Michigan, besides affording a good night's rest in a large airy state-room on board one of Goodrich's magnificent side-wheel steamers FREE OF CHARGE, thereby saving sleeping-car fare and being free from the dust of Railway summer travel.

Passenger cars are equipped with the Westing House air-brake. The track is laid throughout with steel rails. Four Express trains daily—East and West. Dr. Horton's celebrated Reclining Chair and Sleeping-Car attached to all through trains.

For information and tickets via this route, apply to all Railroad Ticket Agents, or to

HARRY BRADFORD, Passenger Ag't, 395 Broadway, Milwaukee, Wis.

J. W. DREW, City Ag't, Rathbun House, Grand Rapids. Or to

J. F. McCLURE,

Ass't Gen'l Ticket Ag't, Detroit.

The most shiftless thing in this world is a Vassar College student taking a bath.

Call the next baby Elaine, after Tennyson's heroine. Then, when she is cross, call her the Madelaine.—*Globe Democrat.*

Carlyle considers children a loan. This is better than considering them together. Much better.—*Danbury News.*

Detroit nearly bursts with vanity over the fact that Mehemet Ali's real name is Detroit.

A man who was fooled into buying a pinchbeck watch called it Faith, because it was without works and therefore dead.

When a young lady offers to hem a cambric handkerchief for a rich bachelor, depend upon it she means to sew in order that she may reap.

DETROIT AND CLEVELAND DAILY LINE

Magnificent Side-Wheel Passenger Steamers,

CITY OF DETROIT,	*NORTHWEST,*
Capt. Wm. McKAY.	Capt. D. A. McLACHLAM.

Leave Detroit, M. C. R. R. Wharf, 10.30 p. m., Daily (except Sunday), to all points in the East and South. No charge for Staterooms! Consult your comfort! Enjoy a good night's rest! Avoid the heat and dust of rail travel! Baggage checked through. Tickets for sale at all railroad ticket offices; on board Steamers; and at Company's office, foot Wayne street, Detroit.

D. CARTER, Manager, Foot Wayne St., Detroit.

Why will young men throw away their time and money attending an inferior institution? GOLDSMITH'S (B & S.) BUSINESS UNIVERSITY, of Detroit, Mich., has no superior, and is not equaled by one in fifty. Students and graduates from nineteen different so-called business colleges and commercial schools located in seven different States, have attended this institution, after attending said institutions from two weeks to six months. They all acknowledge their great mistake in not entering this institution in the first place, saving time and money thereby, and getting superior instruction. The counting-house system of actual business, the best ever introduced, is used at this institution, requiring a bank, business offices, board of trade, etc., giving it facilities for obtaining a knowledge of accounts, business papers and business customs not possessed by any similar institution.

Those wishing to enter a Business College where a thorough practical business education can be obtained, should ask the business men of Detroit where it can best be had.

College paper mailed free.

The man who has been looking for a sea serpent all summer has returned and is looking for an oyster in a church fair stew.

Banks may "bust" and "go up" but we defy them to get any of our money to soar with. We deposit our spare change with delinquent subscribers and none of them will ever go up.—*Whitehall Times.*

When you detect clove in the breath, look out for the cloven foot.

He was a well-meaning man, but they had been married a long while, and when he playfully asked her what was next to nothing, she sarcastically answered that at this season of the year she thought his winter flannels were.—*Norwich Bulletin.*

HEALTH LIFT!

Parlors at No. 119 Griswold St., Moffat Block, Detroit.

The Opinions of well known Citizens of Detroit, concerning the merits of the Health Lift.

THE EVENING NEWS in its issue of January 15th, 1878 published a three-column article concerning the Health Lift, which contained the results of interviews with twelve of the leading citizens of Detroit. From this article the following extracts have been taken; and although no attempt is made to preserve the connection, they will fairly illustrate the spirit of the whole:

David Carter.

When THE NEWS man called at the office of the Detroit & Cleveland steamboat company, foot of Shelby street, and inquired for Mr Carter, Mr. Henderson politely gestured with his thumb in the direction all reporters expect to go, and said, "He's up there, lifting." Ascending the stairs, and accepting a proffered chair, a "what's this?" accompanied by an indicating motion of the foot, was answered by Mr. Carter's, "Oh! that is my Health Lift machine. I used to lift at Farnsworth's rooms, in the Moffat Block, but finally bought a machine for my own use."

"What do they ask for them?"

"I paid seventy-five dollars for this."

"Have you used it long?"

"About a year."

"How do you like it?"

"It is the best thing I have ever tried in the way of exercise."

"Isn't that putting it a trifle *strong?*"

"Not a bit. Feel of that!" and an arm was offered that showed a superior muscular development. "I owe the most of that to this. Why, I can lift 675 lbs., and I take it that that is a fair lift for a man of my build."

"Couldn't you get all the exercise you need by walking down from your residence?"

"Not exactly. Walking develops only part of the body, but this seems to effect and stimulate every portion of the system."

"Can you find time to attend to it?"

"It doesn't take much time; not more than ten or fifteen minutes a day, and I feel enough better after exercising to think that I had saved time instead."

George H. Smith,

The senior member of the well-known book firm of E. B. Smith & Co., has not given himself to book knowledge alone, but has judiciously accumulated an amount of muscle that is astonishing when one considers the space available for its accommodation. "I am not so large as some others," he said, "but I have frequently lifted 675 pounds on one of the Health Lifts."

"Don't you think it strains and hurts you to lift so much?"

"I didn't do it the *first* time I lifted. I began low and gradually worked up into the heavy weights."

"Has Mr. Farnsworth any special scale of weights to be lifted from day to day?"

"The New York manufacturers issue printed tables that are carefully graded and adapted to any desired weight. The rule is not to advance more than five pounds per day."

"You like it, then?"

"Yes."

"In what *way* do you feel a benefit?"

"It broadens and strengthens my chest and I feel stronger and in better health."

"Any other way?"

"My wife notices and remarks it if I skip a day."

"How so?"

"Oh! if I don't lift I am apt to feel inclined to lie down on the sofa and rest after dinner, and she notices that I don't feel as well as on the days I lift."

"That's singular."

"Its a simple fact, and I would as soon account for it some other way, if I could, but I can't.

C. R. Mabley.

"Mr. Mabley, are you prepared to raise your right hand and solemnly swear that you think this Health Lift exercise *pays?*"

"I *know* it does. I *know* it does!"

"How do you *know* it?"

"Because—I'll tell you. In the first place I don't have much time to spare, and I can step over here any time, and I am not away from business more than 20 minutes a day."

"Well."

"Then a man *needs* something of the kind, and this seems to exactly fill the bill."

"Have you given it a fair trial?"

"I think so. This is my second quarter, and I am having my daughter exercise too. She likes it, and I think it is a capital thing for her.

M. S. Smith.

Mr. Smith has a private office in the front of the floor above his jewelry salesroom, so arranged that above a neat gas-log grate in the corner is an obliquely arranged mirror, which shows the whole interior of the room to the one occupying the chair behind the screen.

Exchanging nods of recognition through the mirror, the reporter passed in, and, appropriating the heat from the grate by unfolding his hands behind him until they prevented any further radiation, he remarked:

"I understand that you are *not* now using the Health Lift that you commenced upon fifteen months ago. Have you any objections to stating why?"

"No, not at all. I have tried a great many kinds of exercise, and have had a private gymnasium built at my house, where I can practice between 6 and 7:30 every morning; for I find that that is about the only time of day I can be able to attend to it regularly."

"Yes, but about the Health Lift?"

"I was going to say—I commenced lifting at Farnsworth's rooms, and was so much pleased and benefited that I bought one of his machines and put it in my gymnasium, but it took up so much room that I was foolish enough to exchange it for one of the little machines that have been sold in in the city, but which are comparatively worthless."

"How so?"

"It seems to be constructed on a wrong principle, for there is no elasticity about it, and it is much inferior to the larger and "reactionary" lift. It is so much inferior that I do not use it at all."

"You refer to the little machines with a stout spiral spring in the handles?"

"Yes?"

"What do you think of the one you traded off?"

"I made a mistake in letting it go. I liked it very much, and should begin the exercise again if I could spare the time."

☞ Strangers are always welcome.

E. B. FARNSWORTH, Manager.

No. 119 Griswold Street, Detroit, Mich.

Manhattan Beach.

NEAR NEW YORK CITY.

WHAT TO SEE THERE.

1. **The Grand Hotel**, the largest of its kind in the world—fronting 660 feet on the ocean—a model of sea-side architecture, unsurpassed in its arrangements for the comfort and convenience of sea-side visitors.

2. **The Great Pavilion**, the finest on the coast. One-half of it is reserved for Picnic Parties, with tables, seats, and attentive waiters free of charge. It has already become famous for its moderate charges and the cuisine of its restaurant, especially its fish dishes.

3. **Surf Bathing** at Manhattan Beach is unequaled. At a cost of $125,000 the finest bathing establishment in existence has been erected and furnished. Manhattan Beach is conceded by all to be the best on the coast. It has a long, gentle slope of firm sand, with no bars, pitfalls or undertow; the surf is even and pleasant, and the temperature of the water delightful. The extensive Laundry, furnished with costly steam washers, wringers and dryers, enables the Bathing Company to keep all articles of dress in the best possible condition, and this is the only bathing establishment where bathing suits are thoroughly cleansed. The suits are carried to the laundry from all parts of the immense establishment by ingenious pneumatic machinery. Life-lines surround the entire bathing grounds, and Life-boats, with experienced sailors, are kept constantly outside for the immediate aid and relief of any bather that may require it. 220,000 people bathed here in 1878 without an accident or the approach to one.

4. **The Ladies'** Bathing Pavilion, exclusively for ladies and children; only female attendants allowed. It has 800 large rooms, and is patronized by an average of over 2,000 ladies daily. All rooms have gas and running water. The elegant ladies' parlor and dressing room, panelled with French mirrors, is something unique in the way of sea-side bathing accommodations. Realizing the fact that many ladies hesitate to bathe by reason of the necessity of elbowing their way to and from the water through crowds of curious people on the beach, we have enclosed THE SPACE DIRECTLY IN FRONT OF THE BUILDINGS FOR BATHERS. To insure perfect order, Policemen constantly patrol this enclosed space. There are also 150 rooms fitted up for hot salt-water baths, where this great luxury and remedial agency can be enjoyed in comfort.

5. **The Gentlemen's** Bathing Pavilion has 1,900 rooms, 1,100 of which have gas and running water. 3,500 persons can bathe at one time. From 2,500 to 12,000 people bathe daily at Manhattan Beach. Immense safes are provided in both Pavilions for safe keeping of valuables without charge; only 25 cents is charged for bathing (suits included)—no more than is charged at the most indifferent place on the coast.

6. **The Amphitheatre** is a beautiful and novel building, free to bathers and children, only 10 cents admission to others. It fronts the bathing grounds, affords a place for watching the bathing in comfort, while listening to music by members of Gilmore's Band, who play in this building daily from 1 to 2.30, 3.30 to 4.30, and 5 to 6.15 P. M.

7. **The Immense Captive Balloon**, similar in size and construction to the great Captive Balloon of Paris, under charge of Prof King, will make daily ascensions from Manhattan Beach to the height of 1,000 feet. It is 65 feet in diameter, and when inflated will stand 90 feet in height. It will be lowered by steam power, and will carry 15 persons. Prof. King will make hourly observations of the air currents, atmospheric density, humidity, &c., preparatory to the construction of a monster balloon in which he proposes to cross the ocean next season, starting from Manhattan Beach.

8. **Gilmore's Band.** Gilmore's famous full military band (50 pieces), the most celebrated band in the United States, engaged at great cost for the entire summer, give grand free open-air concerts every afternoon and evening, from 3 to 5 and from 6 30 to 9 p.m.

9. **The Far-Famed "Levy,"** indisputably the greatest Cornet player in the world, will play several selections at each concert. The summer-night concerts at Manhattan Beach cannot be surpassed in the United States. Such a combination as "Gilmore's Band" and "Levy," has never been attempted before at any watering place in this country. For 50 cents one can go from New York City to Manhattan Beach and return, and listen to two concerts that could not be heard elsewhere at less than $1.50 each.

10. **The Marine Railway.** A lovely ride along the entire front of the magnificent estate belonging to the Manhattan Beach Company. Fare from the hotel grounds to the East End and return (four miles), 10 cents. Fare between Manhattan Beach Hotel and the west end of its property (near Hotel Brighton), 5 cts.

11. **The East End.** At the extreme east end of Manhattan Beach there is a pleasant Pavilion, affording the most delightful views of the Ocean, Sheepshead Bay, Rockaway and the many islands of Jamaica Bay. The restaurant is fully supplied with all delicacies of the season, especially fresh fish, just caught, and the prices are very moderate. A regular Rhode Island Clam-bake is ready here every day at 5 P. M. Trains run every ten minutes.

12. **The Boat House and Landing.** At the East End there is always in waiting a fleet of row boats, sailing vessels and fishing yachts with experienced sailors. This landing is but a few hundred feet from the Ocean, giving fishing parties ready access to the outside fishing grounds, and in fifteen minutes the fishing at Jamaica Bay can be reached, and there are no better fishing grounds on this coast than here. The "East End" is certain to become the great rendezvous for New York and Brooklyn, for fishing, yachting, sailing and rowing parties and clubs.

13. **500 Acres of Sea Beach.** Not least in point of attraction is this grand area of sea beach—with its ocean-front of 2½ miles. The Company propose to improve and beautify this natural "Ocean-Park," by constructing lakes and artificial canals—enclosing the whole within a water-tight dyke, and encircling it all with an extension of the Marine Railway—so that visitors can enjoy the novelty of riding six miles in a circular sea-side railway, giving them exquisite views of Bay and Ocean. The Company has determined never to sell or lease a foot of their property, but will erect other hotels, cottages, and improve and beautify the grounds for the exclusive use and enjoyment of their patrons.

14. **The Wonderful Electric Lights**—to be introduced this season—the most expensive kind in the United States, throw a flood of brilliant light over the grounds, buildings and water The beautiful and novel effect of these lights playing upon the waves and surf is indescribable.

"A prudent man," says a witty Frenchman "is like a pin; his head prevents him going too far."

Barnum told the people of London that he had to lecture because his wife spent so much money. He gave her audience next day. He has not been heard of since, and it is feared that he has met with some accident.

"Waiter," he yelled with an awful roar, "This napkin, I'm sure, has been used before." "By four, sir, no," did the waiter say—"You're only the third that's used it to-day."

A visitor to an art-gallery on being asked whether he preferred pictures to statuary, said he preferred the latter, as "you kin go all round statoos, but you see only one side of the picters."

The Queen's Hotel,

TORONTO.

THE QUEEN'S is one of the largest and most comfortable Hotels in the Dominion of Canada: and being adjacent to the Lake, commands a splendid view of Toronto Bay and Lake Ontario. It is well known as one of the coolest houses, in Summer, in Canada, and is elegantly furnished throughout: rooms "en suite," with bath-rooms, etc., attached on every floor.

In 1871, a suite of apartments was occupied by His Imperial Highness, the Grand Duke Alexis of Russia.

His Excellency, the Earl of Dufferin, K. P., etc., etc., Governor-General of Canada, and the Countess of Dufferin, on the occasion of each visit to Toronto, engaged apartments at the QUEEN'S.

The beautiful grounds about it being both spacious and airy, with Croquet and Chevalerie Lawns, render it one of the most pleasant and desirable Hotels for business men, pleasure seekers and the traveling public.

Terms for Board, per day, $2.50 to $3.50, according to location of rooms. Bath-rooms, etc., attached, $1.50 per day extra.

For the convenience of the guests, a Passenger Elevator has been added to the Hotel during the past season.

AMERICAN PLAN.

OTTAWA HOTEL,

MONTREAL.

The Only First Class Hotel near the Public Buildings and Objects of Interest.

Situated on James Street—the Broadway of Montreal.

☞ Passenger Elevator, Modern Furniture, and all the Comforts of a First Class Hotel.

KINGSLEY HOUSE,

OPPOSITE INTERNATIONAL HOTEL,

Falls Street, Niagara Falls, New York.

ADJOINING RUSSIAN AND TURKISH BATH PARLORS.

Meals Served at all Hours. - Terms, $1.50 per Day.

Special inducements to parties continuing any length of time.

Mrs. F. W. KINGSLEY, Proprietress.

No expression of the human countenance can equal the look of lonesome amazement that flashes over the face of the solitary oyster at finding himself scooped up in a gallon of church sociable soup.—*Burlington Hawkeye.*

Farragut was lashed to the mast, and a shoe peg is mashed to the last. Singular coincidence *Worcester Press.*

Great Britain paid over $700,000,000 for intoxicating drinks in 1875. It cannot be told how much America paid in the same time, so much of it was charged.—*Danbury News.*

So many hotel clerks have gone into bankruptcy in Philadelphia since the Centennial that a very fine cluster diamond pin can be had there from fifteen cents down.

The THOUSAND ISLAND HOUSE,

ALEXANDRIA BAY, N. Y.

O. G. STAPLES, - - - - - PROPRIETOR.

THE THOUSAND ISLAND HOUSE

Is well known as not only the most commodious and sumptuously kept hotel on the St. Lawrence River, but also as being located amid some of the grandest scenery in the country, standing, as it does, on the immediate borders of the far-famed Thousand Islands. It is by far the most convenient as well as the most desirable place in many other respects, for the headquarters of all who desire to avail themselves of the pure air, the excellent sport, the grand scenery and the general attractions of this popular resort.

FOR THE SEASON OF 1879,

The proprietor of the Thousand Island House has labored diligently, sparing neither effort nor expense, to render his hotel more attractive, and more desirable in all those nameless points which go to make up the first-class, popular house.

The hotel itself which accommodates 700 guests, the lofty tower of which overlooks 500 of the beautiful Islands of the St. Lawrence, is now equipped and furnished throughout in the most perfect manner; and many desirable improvements, all tending to make the stay of guests more pleasant and satisfactory, have been added.

The variety and grandeur of the scenery in this locality, the wonderful health-giving character of the atmosphere, the beneficial effects of the mineral waters from the great spring which has recently been secured by the proprietor of the Thousand Is and House, and the excellent sporting all conspire to render this the summer Eldorado of men, women and children from all parts of the country. To provide suitable, comfortable, homelike, and at the same time sumptuous accommodations for all who will, during the present season, make this their Mecca, has been the ardent desire of the proprietor of the Thousand Island House; and he is willing to state with confidence that he has succeeded.

THE OFFICE

Is in charge of Mr. R. Patten, late of the R. R. Eating House, Utica, N. Y., a gentleman well known as an obliging and affable person.

THE DINING ROOM

Is under the supervision of Mr. F. J. King, late of the Delevan Hotel, Albany, will seat 500 people, is elegantly frescoed, and pronounced the finest room in the State. The fact that the celebrated

Chef de Cuisine, Edward Loeffke, from the Grand Central Hotel, N. Y.

With a corps of experienced assistants, has been engaged by the management, is a sufficient guarantee that the already well established reputation of the table of this house will be more than maintained.

An elegant Croquet Lawn adjoins the hotel; and a commodious Bowling Alley and Shooting Gallery have also been added for the comfort and amusement of the guests.

THE HOTEL MAY BE REACHED

From New York via Hudson River Railroad or People's Line of Boats to Albany, thence by New York Central Railroad to Rome and Rome, Watertown and Ogdensburg Railroad to Cape Vincent, thence by the new and beautiful steamer "Island Belle," to Alexandria Bay. Or from Utica via Utica and Black River Railroad to Clayton, connecting with the fine steamer "Kelly," arrive at Clayton at 9.35 A. M., Alexandria Bay at 10.35 A. M. From the West, visitors connect at Syracuse with Rome, Watertown and Ogdensburg Railroad, or via Niagara Falls, Rochester and Charlotte, thence by Royal Mail steamers direct to Alexandria Bay. From Ogdensburg by the steamer "Stranger," Capt. Hanna, in connection with A. M. trains on Ogdensburg and Lake Champlain R. W., and St. Lawrence and Ottawa R. R.

The proprietor thanks the public for the generous patronage of the past, and hopes for a continuance of its favors.

Send two 3-cent stamps for Illustrated Pamphlet with diagram of rooms.

O. G. STAPLES, Proprietor.

At Natchez, the other day, a stray sheep accidently fell into the hold of a coal barge. Coaled wether down there.—*N. Y. Commercial Advertiser.*

A little boy came to his mother recently and said: "Mamma, I should think if I was made of dust I should get muddy inside when I drink coffee."

The way the King of the Sandwich Islands carves a chicken is to take hold of both legs, draw a long breath and pull for all he is worth. *Detroit Free Press.*

A teamster who carelessly drove a cart full of building stones over a pedestrian excused himself on the plea that it was not his cart, and he didn't know it was loaded.

CAPE COTTAGE,

PORTLAND, ME.

Is the nearest watering place to the city of Portland, being only three miles distant, a picturesque and pleasant drive.

The building has just been thoroughly rebuilt, refitted, and refurnished, rendering it one of the best and pleasantest as well as most home-like of any house in the vicinity.

It would be difficult to imagine anything more picturesque than the location of CAPE COTTAGE.

The house is surrounded by grassy knolls and hollows, beyond which, in front is an array of ragged cliffs and sunken ledges, about which the breakers are forever toiling, coming direct from the ocean, which stretches on without a break to the horizon.

On the left is the main entrance to Portland Harbor, and every vessel of magnitude which enters or leaves the port passes in full sight. In the distance are the outer islands of Casco Bay.

This house will be kept in first-class style in every particular, and permanent boarders, transient guests, and parties will be furnished with the best accommodations at moderate prices.

This house will be opened on the FIRST DAY OF MAY for the reception of visitors.

Carriages to and from Portland, and to all railroads and steamboats.

Address,

FRANK L. FOSS & CO., *Proprietors*,

PORTLAND, MAINE.

Marriage increases a man's modesty so that after a year or two he can't summon up enough courage to kiss the woman whose lips in the vanishing past, were glued to his four hours on a stretch three times a week.—*Fallon Times.*

The "Lady Slipper" is the name of a vessel just launched at Boston. She must be intended for the whaling service.

We can generally tell what a man's going to do next, when he puts the lighted end of a cigar into his mouth by mistake.

A smart school boy says it takes thirteen letters to spell cow, and proves it thus: "See O! double you."—*Yonkers Gazette.*

The man who said he was "out on a lark" was really out on a swallow.

OLD ORCHARD HOUSE,

ESTABLISHED 1840.—HOUSE BURNT 1875.—RE-BUILT 1876.

PATRONS of Summer Sea-Side Resorts will find no place on the New England Coast with more attractions and comforts than OLD ORCHARD BEACH, Maine. It is at the mouth of the Saco River, on the Boston & Maine Railroad, one hundred miles east from Boston and fifteen miles west from Portland. The inland scenery in the vicinity is varied and pleasing, and the Beach, the finest on the American Coast, presents at low tide, a smooth, solid sand surface for many miles, affording Driving and Bathing facilities unequalled.

To accommodate the numerous patrons of this popular place, there are twenty hotels and boarding-houses, the principal of which is the

OLD ORCHARD HOUSE,

Which will be opened for guests after June 1st, 1879. This Hotel has better accommodations than any sea-side house in New England. Five hundred guests can be conveniently entertained. The private apartments are especially furnished for convenience and comfort. Each room is illuminated with gas, and communication can be held directly with the office by means of Creighton's Oral Annunciator.

Orchestral music is in attendance in the spacious Entertainment Hall during the pleasure season, and for the accommodation of private theatricals there is a stage fitted with drop-curtains and scenery.

A cheerful and commodious Billard Hall is furnished with three elegant modern Tables.

A skilful Physician resides in the House.

The Office is connected with the Western Union Telegraph.

In the vicinity is FERN PARK and the beautiful Grove of the Methodist Camp-Meeting Association, where religious service is held every Sabbath.

An Excellent Livery and Boarding Stable is under the management of the Hotel.

E. C. STAPLES, Proprietors.

There is, once in a while, a woman in this country who thinks that "household management" stops at the making of a worsted dog.—*Detroit Free Press.*

A Sunday-school class in Wilmington was asked who was the author of the Psalms. Silence, at first; then a little hand was held up. "I know." "Who?" "Sam."

One of Milwaukee's druggists has a brand of peculiarly tenacious leeches which he calls "the postmaster leeches." He says they all have to be pulled off.

The reason why a lightning-rod agent creeps into a feather-bed during a thunder shower is because he has such a load of old iron on his conscience.—*Rome Sentinel.*

A SIDE-TRIP UP THE SAGUENAY.

———o———

The members of Mr. Brearley's special Excursion Party are respectfully invited to avail themselves of the reduced rate offered for their benefit, for a trip to the majestic and sublime

SAGUENAY RIVER,

Which remains unrivaled in this world for its grand and impressive scenery. No one should miss this trip. The elegant passenger steamers "St. Lawrence," "Union" and "Saguenay," will leave Quebec as per specially advertised dates, in the morning at 6 o'clock, proceeding down the picturesque St. Lawrence, calling at Murray Bay, River du Loup and Tadousac, the noted seaside resorts of Canada; up the Saguenay River at night, returning down the Saugenay by DAYLIGHT, giving an opportunity of seeing every *mile* of entire route.

This magnificent trip, occupying 48 hours, is offered to members of Mr. Brearley's party, including meals and state-room berth, for $10.00.

Apply early for accommodation to

W. H. BREARLEY.

GUSTAVE LEVE, Gen. Agt. for U.S. of Saguenay Line Steamers, offices opposite St. Louis Hotel, Quebec, and 271 Broadway, New York.

PORTRAITS, ETC.,
BUILDINGS AND LANDSCAPES,
MACHINERY OF ALL KINDS,
LABELS, PLAIN AND COLORED.

SHOW CARDS,
POSTERS IN COLORS,
CATALOGUE ILLUSTRATIONS,
FINE BOOK WORK,
CIRCULARS, MONOGRAMS, ETC.

It was a Long Island boy who, when his mother was pelting him with a shingle, expressed a wish to go back of the returning board.

A dealer advertises "A large stock of bankrupt pianos and organs." Now, who would wish to purchase musical instruments whose notes were not good.—*Detroit Free Press.*

The following dialogue was overheard the other day: He—'Araminta, *je t'adore.*" She—"Shut it yourself."

New Cook: "If you're going up stairs, Mr. Ruggles, you might just tell my lady that if she c'n't write the 'Menoo' in French, I shall be very 'appy to do it for her!"—*Punch.*

It hardly looks well for Alexis to be buying $200 dogs while his father is looking around to borrow money.—*Danbury News.*

Did you ever wake up in the night and muse upon what a nice eternal fitness there is about all things? Scissors came into use three centuries before the art of printing was discovered. Progress understands her business.

The young woman who said kissing was like a sewing machine, because it seemed so good, evidently alluded to a sewing machine with a feller.

A young lady was asked upon her return from church, last Sunday, what the text was, to which she unhesitatingly replied, "Blessed are the dressmakers."

Drive through Cedar Island and Clark Hill Islands

—TO THE—

BURNING SPRING!

This is the newest and most beautiful drive at Niagara. Five bridges are crossed before reaching the Spring, two of which are Suspensions, spanning 250 feet each. The drive which is about half a mile from the Falls to the Spring, after passing through Cedar Island, follows close to the edge of the Rapids till it reaches the first suspension bridge at Clark Hill Islands. From these Islands—a group of five, is obtained

THE FINEST VIEW OF THE RAPIDS.

The second Suspension Bridge crosses from the Islands to the Spring over

The Fastest Current in the River,

The water flowing at the rate of 27 miles per hour.

THE BURNING SPRING IS ONE OF

The Greatest Natural Curiosities

IN THE WORLD,

And has been too well known for the past 50 years as a great feature at Niagara to need any description here.

☞ Interesting experiments will be shown the visitor at the Spring.

It is folly to pay forty cents for a sheet of music when you can go to church and get it by the choir for nothing.

"Good morning, Donelly! I hear your daughter has a baby; is it a boy or a girl?" "Shure, Miss, it's meself as doesn't yet know for the life of me if I'm a grandfather or a grandmother, bedad."—*London Fun.*

The click of the mallet is again heard on the lawn, and any one who says croquet is going out of fashion is a conspicuously bad player, or else wears No. 6 gaiters.

The foolish man will ask a woman if her baby is not a trifle crosseyed; but the wise man will take the cars to the next town and make his inquiries by postal card.

SUMMER RESORT.

BEEBE HOUSE.

HENRY BEEBE, PROPRIETOR.

PUT-IN-BAY ISLAND, LAKE ERIE, OHIO.

THE BEEBE HOUSE.

Now open under the management of Henry Beebe, has steadily grown in public favor. Last season and this, extensive and modern improvements were made, and it now has comfortable accommodation for 400 guests. The rooms are large and airy, all lighted by coal gas. The offices and dining rooms are spacious, well-lighted apartments, and the latter can seat 400 guests. The *cuisine* needs no recommendation to former patrons, and it is sufficient to say that the reputation of the house will be sustained in this respect. A large building, remote enough from the main structure to prevent annoyance, but connected by walks, is devoted entirely to pleasure. It contains a fine Billiard Room, Bowling Alleys, Ice Cream and Wine Rooms. On the second floor is a spacious Dancing Hall, Ladies' and Gentlemen's Parlors, leading from which are Dressing Rooms, etc

A Barber Shop, Laundry and Livery stable are among the conveniences.

The location, with the lake only a few feet in front, a splendid grove on the left, the only bathing beach on the Island but a short distance in the rear, is one that is not equaled by any other hotel on the Island. The chief charm of the house is, however, its home-like comfort and elegance—two things so seldom found at watering-place hotels—and guests may be assured that they will receive every attention that will make their stay pleasant and agreeable in every respect.

A fine orchestra will be in constant attendance to furnish music for serenades, hops, parties, etc. The popular price, $14 per week. Transient, $2.50 per day.

A good Physician is established upon the Island.

TRAVELING DIRECTIONS.

Visitors from Cincinnati of South can take the C. H. & D. R. R. via Toledo, and thence via Steamer to the Island; or the Short line via Dayton, Springfield and Sandusky, thence via Steamer to the Island. Indianapolis and further West can take the C. C. C. & I. (Bee Line) via Bellefontaine, thence via Short Line to Sandusky. St Louis and all intermediate points can take the O. & M., or Vandalia Line, connecting at Cincinnati with Dayton Short Line, or C. H. & D. R. R. for Sandusky or Toledo. For Peoria and Fort Wayne, Toledo, Wabash & Western, to Toledo.

Baltimore, Philadelphia, Washington and intermediate points can take the B. & O. thence to Sandusky. Columbus can take the C. C. C. & I. or B. & O. R. R. direct to Sandusky.

From Chicago, take the Lake Shore & Michigan Southern, or Michigan Central, to Detroit or Toledo.

From Buffalo and East, take Lake Shore and Michigan Southern to Cleveland or Sandusky, or boat direct.

The Steamer Alaska leaves the dock at the foot of Griswold street, Detroit, daily at 8.30 A. M., and returns at 11 P. M.

"Died of hard drink" was the verdict of an intelligent jury upon the body of a man killed by a falling icicle.—*New York Commercial Advertiser.*

When a visitor enters the sanctum it is better than a whole sermon on human nature to see the editor, with a beautiful air of unconsciousness, slip all the lead pencils into a drawer and put the penknife into his pocket.

When a couple go abroad on their bridal tour, could you call it a marrytime excursion.—*N. Y. Com. Adv.*

It is true that flowers and vegetables are divided into sexes, and it is also true, strange as it may appear, that they have a language of their own. You surely have heard of Jack and the Bean's talk.—*Atlanta Constitution.*

"The slumber of the pure is sweet," says the Talmud. That accounts for sleeping in church, surrounded by the pewrest influences.—*Graphic.*

"Young man," said he solemnly, "I'm sorry to see you smoking tobacco," and the young man assured him that he wasn't—that it was a Connecticut cigar.

It is said that Eve was made for Adams Express Company, but this is probably a figment of some common carrier of slander.—*Cincinnati Enquirer.*

Brigham Young lost his opportunity when he did not write a work entitled "those wives of mine."

www.ingramcontent.com/pod-product-compliance
Lightning Source LLC
Chambersburg PA
CBHW020329090426
42735CB00009B/1457
9783337316556